INSPIRING WRITING THROUGH DRAMA

Also available from Bloomsbury

Getting the Buggers to Write (3rd edition)
Sue Cowley

School Improvement Through Drama
Patrice Baldwin

With Drama in Mind (2nd edition)
Patrice Baldwin

INSPIRING WRITING THROUGH DRAMA

Creative Approaches to Teaching Ages 7–16

Patrice Baldwin and Rob John

B L O O M S B U R Y

LONDON · NEW DELHI · NEW YORK · SYDNEY

First published 2012 by
Bloomsbury Education

An imprint of Bloomsbury Publishing Plc
50 Bedford Square, London, WC1B 3DP
175 Fifth Avenue, New York, NY10010

www.bloomsbury.com

British Library Cataloguing-in-Publication Data
A catalogue record for this book is available from the British Library.

ISBN: 978-1-4411-5909-0 (paperback)
978-1-4411-5511-5 (ePub)
978-1-4411-7022-4 (PDF)

Library of Congress Cataloging-in-Publication Data
Baldwin, Patrice.
Inspiring writing through drama : creative approaches to teaching
ages 7-16 / Patrice Baldwin and Rob John.
p. cm.
Includes bibliographical references and index.
ISBN 978-1-4411-5909-0 – ISBN 978-1-4411-5511-5 – ISBN 978-1-4411-9565-4 –
ISBN 978-1-4411-7022-4   1. English language–Composition and exercises–
Study and teaching–Great Britain.   2. Playwriting–Study and teaching–Great Britain.
3. Drama in education–Great Britain.   4. Role playing.   I. John, Rob, 1950-   II. Title.

LB1576.B257 2012
808'.042071–dc23
2012004196

Typeset by Newgen Imaging Systems Pvt Ltd, Chennai, India
Printed and bound in Great Britain

Contents

PART 2   DRAMA UNITS

PART 3 WRITING RESOURCES

Foreword

At a time when so many aspects of education are becoming more mechanistic, mundane and anaesthetic, this book presents a robust argument in favour of a creative approach to the development of literacy. As its title proclaims, its project is to inspire writing through drama. It seems to me that it certainly delivers what it says on the tin! Following a thorough and thoughtful exposition of the relationship between drama and writing, the book provides a plethora of practical strategies and excellent resources which have been carefully and imaginatively structured to promote the development of both written and oral communication. The richness of the ideas presented here is a celebration of the richness of our language, the fluidity of which is as astonishing as its capacity to evolve.

It has been estimated that Chaucer had a working vocabulary of around 8,000 words. Just 200 years later, Shakespeare was using some 24,000 words. Such a rapid expansion may be put down to the explosion of discoveries emerging from the renaissance. New discoveries and new ideas need new words. Today, the *Oxford English Dictionary* states that there are currently over 170,000 words in common usage. What's intriguing is that not only is the language still expanding, its forms are mutating so we have whole new modes of communication. Not so long ago we might have said that written language could be divided between prose and poetry. Spoken language could be categorized as conversation, narration, recitation and formal, rehearsed speech. And there were hybrid forms in which spoken language was captured in the written word: transcription, for example, and of course dramatic literature. It is here, in these hybrid forms, that the mutation of language has been so prevalent in recent years. We may now add text messaging, emails, blogs and tweets to the list of those forms of writing that draw on and readily reflect the directness and ellipsis of speech. Some of these new modes even employ new forms of notating visual aspects of live oral communication through devices such as emoticons and, lol, textspeak! How then might we embrace the exciting possibilities of our propensity to communicate in new and creative ways while ensuring that what we communicate is worthwhile and effective? Well, 'Inspiring Writing Through Drama' isn't a bad place to start.

When Alexander Pope wrote that 'True ease in writing comes from art, not chance' I suspect he was referring to the care and the craft, the feeling and mastery of form that underpins the most effective manifestations of notated language. In this timely new book, Patrice Baldwin and Rob John not only embrace Pope's aphorism but add another dimension. Neither Patrice nor Rob are slouches when it comes to exercising their own considerable ability to write clearly, purposefully and with feeling. They are both experts in the teaching of drama as a discrete subject. They both have a firm grasp on how to use the art form as a means of exploring the whole curriculum in order to help develop children's knowledge, skills and understanding of a wide spectrum of human experience. And they both have an impressive amount of expertise in working with teachers, encouraging them to extend their range of teaching strategies and work alongside the budding artists who are their pupils. In short, they are both wholly committed to the concept and practice of drama for learning and fostering creativity. In this book they draw on their own classroom experience and related theory to present a convincing case for the integration of drama, speaking, listening, reading and writing in the development of literacy. Their case is bolstered by the voices of teachers and pupils who have seized the moment and recognized the potential of working in this integrated way. The resulting wisdom, advice, guidance and wealth of practical ideas delineated in this book are most certainly the product of art, not chance.

But what of the extra dimension they have added to Pope's apothegm? Quite simply, the key to the authors' thesis is that children will find true ease in writing if that writing comes from their engagement with the art of drama. It would be hard to argue with their dictum that, 'the cornerstone of literacy is speaking and listening. Before children can read or write, they need first to be able to speak.' Chomsky famously postulated that our initial acquirement of language occurs through an innate 'language acquisition device'. So, lucky old us! We don't really have to try too hard to learn how to speak: so long as we are spoken to as children, we'll just pick it up! However, as Patrice and Rob point out, 'not all children come to school with rich experiences of speaking and listening.' Furthermore, learning how to notate that language (i.e. putting squiggles on a page to represent the sounds of speech) and learning how to decode those squiggles (i.e. reading and comprehending them) demand skills that are far from innate. In some ways both reading and writing may be regarded as entirely mechanical. Indeed, we now have machines that can turn the spoken word into print and back again. Does that mean machines are literate? Can they capture and convey the emotion and nuance of a carefully chosen sequence of words whether they be spoken or written? I think not yet. This is where the next part of Patrice and Rob's premise comes in. In order to be truly literate, the ability to read and write responsively and reflectively must be nurtured. This involves learning how to 'listen responsively and reflectively to others and be listened responsively to'. And that's what drama is all about. The essential ingredient of the art of drama is the relationship between speaker/actor and audience. For the one there must be a purpose and motivation to communicate; for the other a reason to listen and watch. If the social experience of interpersonal communication through both the spoken or written word is to be meaningful and worthwhile, then it is certainly not down to chance, but art.

I congratulate Rob and Patrice on what they have achieved in this book. 'Inspiring Writing Through Drama' has every chance of success because the thinking and practice on which it is grounded is inspiring.

Andy Kempe
University of Reading, UK
November 2011

Acknowledgements

This book is dedicated to the many hundreds of teachers and thousands of children and young people, whom we have taught and learned from over many years.

Introduction

This book sets out to inspire and support teachers and in turn help them to inspire and support the children they teach to be writers and 'players' (playful actors in imagined worlds) through well-structured whole-class dramas. It is aimed primarily at teachers and other educators of children and young people who are aged 7–16. We refer to this group collectively as children or pupils throughout the book.

Most Early Years teachers seek opportunities for moving alongside young children 'in role' and supporting and guiding their dramatic role play and their writing in imagined worlds. They know the difference an empathetic adult in role can make and the way that children will engage enthusiastically and confidently when writing within a role play. So why stop developing this as children get older? Why not work alongside older and much older children in imagined worlds as teachers, with a writing agenda for the children? The approach still works at any age and can become very sophisticated.

Drama for writing can be developed continuously and progressively at any age and in any educational setting, but most teachers lack the confidence and experience to use this approach. This book aims to help teachers to become more confident in their use of drama for writing by presenting a rationale for its use, and providing well-structured drama units for teachers to try with their own classes.

Drama with a writing purpose is an underutilized and underdeveloped approach in most primary and secondary schools, and yet drama undoubtedly can help improve most children's writing. For children who lack ideas for writing and/or need lived experiences to help them to get started, this approach is almost a necessity.

Most teachers have tried out a few basic drama strategies to enliven English lessons at some point in their career, and examples can be found in many classrooms of children's writing that has been positively influenced by drama. Rarely, however, is whole-class drama developed enough to maximize what it can bring to writing. Despite some 'hot-seating' and 'freeze frame' in English lessons, too many teachers and children in classrooms remain stubbornly and unnecessarily desk bound for much of the time.

With high stakes assessment, examinations and inspections dominating classroom practice, and with a strong emphasis on teachers having good class control and ensuring good pupil behaviour, there is a tendency for teachers to play it safe, to be risk averse and to overuse the more static and controlling drama activities (often using drama long enough to kick-start the writing). This easily leads to children being short changed creatively and they may start to see drama as just something they do a bit of before writing. This can be very frustrating for children and seriously undervalues and underutilizes the visual, auditory, kinaesthetic and aesthetic nature of drama and its enormous potential for motivating, inspiring and helping provide structure and content for powerful and highly effective writing. Teachers need to be braver, take some calculated risks drama-wise and evaluate the anticipated and unexpected outcomes for the children and for themselves as teachers.

Drama is a powerful, structured and highly effective medium through which teachers can 'marry expression with structure, articulation with feeling/thought and a range of linguistic competence with depth and engagement and imagination' (DCSF 2008). This book offers meaningful and sustained whole-class drama experiences within which a plethora of carefully placed writing opportunities are woven into the drama units. Each one is designed to inspire and motivate children as writers and as drama 'players' and productive creators. The drama units offer integrated reading, speaking, listening and writing activity (as good English teaching demands), but attention should also be paid to the importance of the drama itself, as an aesthetic art form and performance medium. Performance involves process and product and is used in parts of all the units as a means of deepening understanding and accessing, creating and communicating meanings actively during the lessons. Drama also links into the children's writing (process and product). Symbiotically, high-quality drama can inspire high-quality writing, and high-quality writing can inspire high-quality drama.

In Part 1 of this book we explain the rationale underpinning drama for writing and analyse how and why it works in practice. The drama units in Part 2 exemplify this practice; providing pretexts, contexts, content, purposes and audiences for writing within the drama. The units set up compelling reasons for children to work creatively 'in role' and to write, together or separately. They exemplify how writing can be central to the drama itself and how reading, writing, speaking and listening can be integrated and flow through the drama process.

The level of practice encouraged and exemplified by this book is far beyond just the use of a drama strategy or two to kick-start a piece of writing or to ring the changes in an otherwise predictable English lesson.

Part 2 of this book presents the reader with a drama toolbox. It groups the drama strategies according to their main purposes in any drama. This will help you when you are planning your own drama. A basic description and explanation of each strategy is offered and you will find it helpful to refer to Drama Strategies for clarification when you are working with the drama units provided, as well as when you start creating your own.

Each drama unit from Part 2 comes with a set of original writing resources found in Part 3 of the book. These have been specifically devised to support you in embedding the units of work. So, not only have we provided you with the drama unit plan, you also now have all the necessary writing resources readily available from the outset. The written resources include school reports, letters, job advertisements, poems, extracts from play scripts, newspaper headlines, extracts from diaries, and give dramatically rooted reasons for the children to produce other multi-modal texts of their own. Teachers may find, that as well as using these writing resources for drama they can also be used for other purposes, as exemplars and writing frames in less dramatic English lessons.

Where we felt that it would be useful and would save you valuable time we have also made these available on the companion website for download or projection onto the whiteboard.

The drama units themselves have been designed to maximize the potential for writing, while also providing a sustained and satisfying drama experience. There are also ample opportunities to create 'performance' from the texts, both the children's own and those provided, in order to make and communicate meaning in an aesthetic and dramatic way, as well as in written form.

The curriculum subject matter of the eight drama units, all of which have been tried and tested with teachers and children, span historical and futuristic themes, political, cultural, civil, social and family issues.

Both of us hope that once you become aware, theoretically and practically, of how motivating and enjoyable drama can be for your children (and for yourself), as well as how effective it can be for improving children's writing, you will use it often and will also inspire other teachers to give it a try too.

Patrice Baldwin and Rob John

The authors of this book have trained drama teachers together for more than 20 years. Between them they bring the perspectives and experiences of a primary teacher, secondary and FE teacher, university lecturer, local authority adviser, Ofsted inspector, Headteacher and Vice Principal of a sixth form college. They are also both professional writers for children and teachers.

PART 1

DRAMA AND WRITING

1 Breathing Life into Writing

Why does writing matter?

Schools are continuously trying to improve children's writing. Time and again 'raise standards in writing' appears (and then reappears) as a priority in school inspection reports and in school improvement and development plans, yet writing standards in many schools remain stubbornly low, fall or become 'stuck' and teachers become perplexed and frustrated by it. To improve writing, schools need to focus first and foremost on how children learn and how they learn to write well, rather than keeping their primary focus on inspections and tests.

Writing is crucially important throughout life (hence the probable reason for the high status assessments of writing) and we need to equip children to write well and with understanding, for a multiplicity of real and useful purposes. A child who cannot write well enough (or thinks they can't), will struggle emotionally and practically in a host of real life situations and be disadvantaged in relation to many employment opportunities.

At first sight, James, a 23-year-old part-time mechanic working at a garden centre (and also helping out in the shop) might seem (like many young adults) to have little need for complex writing skills. He is dyslexic and his predictions for GCSE were all very low, so he transferred early to do a land-based engineering course at an agricultural college. Practically he is very skilled but struggles emotionally and practically with writing tasks and the written aspects of this course distressed him. James also has a poor short-term memory and he needs job lists to follow but is very capable at the mechanical jobs. He forgets what jobs he has to do without lists (to the extreme irritation of some past employers). In his current job James needs daily to write his own lists of the jobs that must be done on various machines. He wrote a CV (with help) when he was at college and learned how to structure a covering letter. He was given a model which he still adapts when necessary. He keeps his CV updated. He sends emails a few times a week to potential employers with his CV attached. If he forgets to spell-check emails they usually have spelling mistakes which would be off putting to most potential employers. He sometimes fills in application forms (which he needs to have checked). James has created a business card and flyers to drop off at local houses in the hope of privately getting some machinery repair jobs. He had to learn recently how to write his first invoice for his first private customer. He buys and sells some garden machinery and a few motorbikes on an internet sales site, so writes adverts and responds in writing to queries. He spends a lot of time every day posting messages on a social networking site and writing on chat walls to his 'friends'. He is highly motivated to chat online, as he sees this writing activity as socially essential. Text messaging too is important to him but the abbreviations etiquette confuses him. He labours over getting the words and tone just right for texts to his girlfriend (and his ex). He keeps a written record of when he is working at home on engines, as a neighbour complained about noise and he wants to record accurately time, length and level of noise in case she formally complains to the council. James keeps an itemized record of his spending and sometimes writes shopping lists. He often writes on his hand to remember things. He is painstaking about the content and legibility of messages he writes in birthday cards. When he was at primary school he used to write very creative stories (although spelling and punctuation was a problem). He never writes stories now but still has a great imagination. James claims now that he never writes.

The modes of writing have changed and will keep changing. Social networking sites and mobile phone texting are writing media that children are often most familiar with and lead a generation of children and young adults to frequently write short and multiple messages (often on screens). Sustained concentration and sustained pieces of writing and narratives are less practiced. Children live in a world of flashing screens and short text and sound bites. The leading UK neuroscientist Susan Greenfield calls today's children the 'yuck and wow' generation and says they have less experience and less developed skills of sustained concentration and narrative. They are presented with many images and have less need to imagine and 'fill in the gaps'. What she says of novels and the Net, could equally be applied to drama.

> A novel is a narrative [with] a beginning, a middle and an end. It takes you through something. Whereas the Net, you pop into it, you pop out of it. There is no obvious narrative line . . . In novels you've got the characters and they are very real, but you don't know what they look like as such, you don't know what their face looks like, you wouldn't necessarily be able to paint them – yet they are very real. (Dreyfus, June 2000)

Networking sites offer us the opportunity to present ourselves, our image, lifestyle and/ or professional activities online (often restricting the number of words or characters), to an unknown and potentially large audience. For many children writing online is driven by social purpose and they therefore get hooked on it. They see social networking as a way of extending and 'bigging up' their 'friendship' groups in an almost competitive way. Within days (or even hours) children can have dozens of shadowy, so-called friends that they have little or no face-to-face social interaction with but have a stilted writing dialogue with instead. Their social needs are being partly met through punchy and quick modes of writing that are not congruent with the broader range of skills and applications they need to also develop to become competent and enthusiastic writers in other real life contexts (including in the workplace).

We don't write letters and cards to friends and relatives as often nowadays, preferring to use emails or phone calls and so sustained, personal forms of writing are less common and less practiced. Modes of writing alter over time but the need to be able to write appropriately and flexibly (and sometimes cautiously) for different purposes and audiences remains.

The internet has also led to many of us (including children and young people) becoming very public as writers. We write easily on blogs and social networking websites and we are now more likely to have our writing abilities judged by others (often without us even knowing who has seen what we have written). We all find ourselves in situations where the first judgement that is being made about us by others is based on something we have written, whether it is a blog, an email, job application, a text or letter of complaint for example. Everyone is a writer, whose writing (in whatever mode) is read by an audience (intended or not) that is expected and likely to respond in some way. We write mainly for response, so we need to help children to become circumspect about what they write to an audience to protect them. Modes of writing will continue to develop and change and children will need to be continuously adaptable and reflective as writers.

In this competitive and assessment driven world, our writing is also being judged and compared to each other's. It matters personally and professionally to us that we feel able to (and can) write at least as well as most other people. If we apply for a job and the letter is not well written, we are disadvantaging ourselves, just as if we write a professional blog and put in inappropriate content we are also not doing ourselves any favours.

Writing can live on through its readers and remain for posterity. Most writing involves some form of creativity and it is an art form. Writing (like drama) is also an important means of sharing, recording and communicating our thoughts and feelings about people, circumstances and events that matter to us and to others. When we write beyond the purely functional, we are often giving of ourselves personally and maybe emotionally. How our writing is received by others matters and can touch our self-esteem and our emotions to our work. If children's writing is criticized carelessly by teachers they can easily feel personally criticized because writing is borne of us and is part of us. If on the other hand our writing is welcomed, praised, appreciated (Figure 1.1), we can be spurred on to still greater effort and feel good about ourselves as writers.

We need to think before we write and conversely, engagement with writing, our own and other people's, helps us to clarify and deepen our thinking. Different types of writing require and help develop different types of thinking. If we are writing a shopping list for example, we may use

Figure 1.1 Writing can be made prominent in drama

logical reasoning, order information, group, prioritize and sequence. If we are writing a poem on the other hand, we may be involved in creative and critical thinking, selecting, synthesizing, ordering, grouping, evaluating and revising. The former may be pragmatic and functional and the latter may be aesthetically pleasing and engage us emotionally. Both are purposeful in their different ways and both types of writing matter at the time. The first will be forgotten in the future, the latter may not as we will be emotionally engaged with it.

The use of word processing has changed the way we write. We can write with the knowledge that editing is more easily and immediately achieved. We can check spelling and easily make alterations at any point in the writing process. We can play with the writing repeatedly and save versions and avoid the sometimes dispiriting and messy scribbling out that writing straight onto paper can entail. Grammatical errors will usually be picked up for us electronically. This does mean that we may be able to get technical aspects of writing correct without necessarily understanding why it was wrong in the first place. Lonesome and efficient word processing is not the same however, as having grammar, punctuation and spelling talked about and explained by an empathetic and knowledgeable teacher. Word processing is a tool, not a substitute for face-to-face teaching and engagement with a teacher who can listen, explain and challenge with sensitivity during the writing process.

What skills and experiences do we need in order to become effective writers?

The cornerstone of literacy is speaking and listening. Before children can read or write, they need first to be able to speak, listen responsively and reflectively to others and be listened responsively to. Through no fault of their own, not all children come to school with rich experiences of speaking and listening. Many children are being expected to read and write when they have poorly developed speaking and listening skills. Some may not have been read to at home and may have a narrow vocabulary bank. Needless to say this is not a good position to start writing. There will be great disparity between the pre-school and later experiences of children as talkers and listeners and this will significantly influence their progress as readers and writers.

Most schools give more attention to planning the teaching of reading and writing than to planning for speaking and listening. There is sometimes a self-limiting assumption made, that children will gradually just 'pick it up' speaking and listening through daily exposure. All children will benefit from learning and practising different ways of speaking effectively and purposefully in different registers for different audiences, for different purposes. They will also benefit greatly from learning how to become active and responsive listeners and being given a range of speaking and listening development and practice opportunities (many of which can be provided through drama).

Young children soon pick up that writing seems to be something very important that they are expected to pay serious attention to. They may have this perplexing thing called a newspaper in their house that parents pay attention to regularly and sometimes read aloud from. They may have these mysterious things called books on shelves (many without pictures) that are full of lines of squiggles and can engross grown-ups for hours. They may start to recognize and connect written and spoken words, when stories are being read aloud to them (often repeatedly) from books that they enjoy. Alternatively of course, they may come from homes where reading for pleasure or information is rarely or never seen, where they are not read to and where they don't see grown-ups reading or writing much (if ever).

Young children start early to imitate adults in many ways through dramatic play. Within their dramatic play, they will often pretend they can write (scribbling), long before they actually can write. This is because their curiosity about writing has been aroused and they want to act out being a grown-up and know what it feels like emotionally and physically to be able to write. There are connections being made between speaking, listening, writing, reading and pleasure in many homes but these can become all too easily disconnected again by schools that separate it all out too much of the time, rather than meaningfully integrating the activities (as drama can).

Children need something that they understand and want to write about. Too often children are asked to write about something that is totally removed from their knowledge, life experiences, imaginations or interests, for example, a typical GCSE type writing task question might be:

> Write a letter to advise your cousin about what to do with the rest of his/her life, since he/she is about to leave school. (Brindle and Richardson 2009)

To engage with this task meaningfully and do it well, I might reasonably feel I need certain information and more context. What is my relationship with my cousin like? What does my cousin actually want to do next? If I am still at school myself, do I have the knowledge, experience and right to advise my cousin about his/her future? Why would/should my cousin pay any attention to me? Would it be more appropriate to phone for a chat first rather than write to my cousin? Do I need to ask my cousin some questions first, to learn more, before I can confidently advise? And so on.

If we bring such a writing task alive for children first and give the pretext and context through drama, then they may want and be able to write successfully to their imaginary cousins. If, for example, pairs of children as cousins were given the situation and asked to chat first in role (maybe on imaginary mobile phones), their improvised dialogue could then provide content and a more accessible pretext for the writing task. Another actual example:

> Write a section for a guide book for visitors to this country, to inform them about what Britain has to offer. (Brindle and Richardson 2009)

I need to be able to prepare well for this task. If I am writing a short section in this book, what are the other sections and how is my section intended to fit in? What is the age group of the visitors I am writing for? Am I to assume they are adults and read English well or must I make the language simple? And so on . . .

If pairs of children improvise as a tourist information employee and a visiting, English-speaking tourist from abroad and discuss for a while the main tourist attractions in Britain, this could lay the foundations for then writing a guide book section (ideally following some actual research into attractions). Also there may need to be some enquiry and online research of tourist attractions necessary before the section of the guide book can be written well. It is not fair or wise to set individual children writing tasks that they do not feel they are equipped to do well, and it can be counterproductive.

Many adults would find these examples of thinly contextualized writing tasks daunting and feel ill equipped to complete them with so little information and engagement (especially if writing in exam conditions). It is fine to ask children to use their imaginations but they are still likely to require some support, some simulated, lived and shared experience that will engage them and provoke an emotional response. They may lack motivation to write if the tasks lack real meaning, value or purpose for them and are outside their real and/or imagined experience.

In order to write, children may need background information but they also need to be able to organize their thoughts first.

→ What do I want to actually say in this writing? (content)

→ Who do I want to say it to? (audience)

→ What do I want the outcome to be? (purpose)

→ How do I need to organize this writing? (organization)

→ What are the best words to use? (vocabulary)

→ Is the grammar and punctuation correct? (grammar and punctuation)

→ Was it fit for purpose? Did it work? (evaluation)

Children need access to good models of different types and genres of writing (some of which the 'Writing Resources' in this book are examples of). You can't write a magazine article or a letter or a poem or a horror story, for example if you don't know what one looks like, have never read one or heard one and don't know what criteria you must meet when constructing one. Again, children need to be shown and helped to analyse different types of writing. Drama is a medium through which types of writing can be introduced within an engaging context. Children can be hooked into a drama that brings with it writing to read and emotionally and socially compelling reasons to write (as the drama requires it).

Several years ago there was a writing task given in a national English standardized attainment test. In test conditions, the nervous children (aged 11) were given written instructions that told them to imagine that they had witnessed a car accident caused by a fox dashing out into the road at night. They were then asked to write about the incident in the form of a police report. An unexpectedly high number of the 'more able' writers did less well than expected at this task. When the writing papers were analysed, they revealed that many children had automatically written a piece of descriptive, creative writing (along similar lines to the piece below).

> The sleek red fox streaked out from behind the gloomy bushes and was immediately bathed in silvery moonlight. As it dashed onto the shadowy road, the startled driver saw it suddenly and swerved in panic . . .

To respond to an official report writing task in this way is clearly inappropriate, so why did they do this? Probably because they had practised creative story writing most and wrote in this way automatically. Maybe they were not able to imagine an accident they did not actually see and that had not been brought alive in some way or maybe they could not imagine themselves to be policemen writing. Drama activity could have provided the role engagement and missing steps that many children probably needed in order to be able to complete the task well.

> There seemed to be an almost seamless run from need, to thought, to speaking, to writing and then back to reading in role. All children were clear about what they had written, including four children who have been working on Individual Education Plans to support their writing, and the three children in the focus group. (A primary teacher action researcher) (D4LC 2005)

Drama will help improve the writing of many children but may be particularly helpful for less able or less imaginative writers, including those on the autistic spectrum who may have particular difficulty imagining and often find it easier to write literally and who find it difficult to write about what they have not actually experienced.

If the children had experienced being in role as a policeman, interviewed an eye witness to an accident (Teacher in Role or TiR), or recreated an accident scene from a text source, then maybe, when faced with a police report task later in a test situation, their report writing would have been more convincing and appropriately written. The class could even have been cast as trainee police officers who needed to improve their report writing and were being directly taught how to before the test. A drama scenario could then have provided an imaginative context for teaching spelling, punctuation and grammar in role! The TiR as a police trainer could be focusing the attention of the trainees on what constitutes good police report writing and the TiR could teach the specific aspects of it. Certainly it is worth teachers trying and considering what difference it makes. Drama easily provides contexts for writing but children still need to learn the technical skills of writing and often these may be best taught directly (although even this can be done in an imaginative, dramatic context). It may seem a bit quirky, a bit 'out of the box' as an approach but it would be interesting, engaging and memorable.

Clearly drama can't take place in a real test situation but learning and practicing writing in drama scenarios can lead to some good report writing (as well as other types of writing) that the children can feel successful about and then remember and draw on more confidently later in a test situation. Schools are increasingly teacher assessing for learning and compiling children's writing portfolios as evidence of children's achievement in writing. It is valid to approach writing through drama and highlight in writing assessment portfolios that drama was the pretext and/ or context for the writing. Writing portfolios can provide comparative evidence of the positive impact of drama on children's writing standards.

> It (drama) helps you write – it's easier to do it and then put it on paper. It (drama) helped me do my Hansel and Gretel book – I knew the story and only had to write it

down . . . I didn't have to think what to write – just how to do it well. (A pupil's voice) (D4LC 2005)

Writing is a manipulative craft with an intended audience, who are open to being manipulated. Children need to experience being manipulated by writers, to become skilfully manipulative as writers themselves. Drama enables writing to be read, understood, emotionally engaged with and spoken aloud in an imagined and living context. It enables participants to experience and gauge the responses of their live audience (who in the case of whole class drama may also be co-participants in the same drama).

Writers need to be able to constantly shift themselves into readers and back again, in order to craft the writing with the reader in mind. Writers start to develop an internal voice that they can almost hear, that gives them a sense of how that writing reads and sounds to an audience. The writing seeks an internal response from the writer and the reader. Through drama, writing can then be brought alive (Figure 1.2) and given an external voice or voices. The writing can provoke affective and cognitive responses within the drama and can also be given an aesthetic form that derives from but goes beyond words in the conveyance of meaning.

Children as writers also need to listen to and practise 'writer talk', as Pie Corbett says 'to develop the habit of reading with a 'writerly eye' and a 'writer's curiosity' (Corbett 2008). They need to hear aloud what a writer is thinking as they write and as writers themselves, contribute their own thinking and ideas aloud during the writing process. Shared and guided writing (and whole class drama for learning) is a structured way of providing children with 'writer talk' opportunities. The teacher may provide or stimulate 'writer talk' and is usually the lynchpin

Figure 1.2 Through drama, writing can be brought alive

and scribe. The teacher is a model, guide, facilitator and mediator present in the build up and at the point of writing. This model can also work well in a drama context, where the teacher is likely to carry out these functions in role. In role, she may for example ask for the children's help with a piece of writing that will have significance for the drama. The children are engaged with the drama and are compelled and propelled by it to help with the writing. The shared task gives an authentic and lively, 'in role' reason for them to engage in 'writer talk', which is often 'writer in role talk'.

What can go wrong when we try to write?

Learning to write is a slow and complex process. It requires knowledge, skills, understanding, time, practice, perseverance, and an 'I can' attitude. Obviously some children learn to write more easily than others and some get more support at home and consistently better teaching.

Ben spontaneously wrote an adventure story and took it school to show his busy teacher. He asked if he could read it to the class but the teacher said there was no time to. She told him to leave it on her desk and she would read it later. When Ben received his writing back next day it was marked with red pen and the teacher had written, 'Well done Ben but don't forget your writing targets. Remember your capitals and full stops.' He has not given the teacher a story since.

Teachers are under a lot of pressure time wise and can unwittingly de-motivate children. They also can be so exam and test focused that they fall too readily into talking about writing targets rather than talking with and about children as writers.

When children are making slow progress in writing, there is a tendency for them to be given more lessons in writing rather than different types of lessons. Children who are struggling may need to have some direct teaching and intervention support in a 'catch up' group but it may be that the child is just not responding well to the way writing is being taught. Different ways of teaching will hold more appeal for particular children and teachers should try a range of approaches in an evaluative way to see what difference it makes. Drama for learning is one approach that will certainly appeal to the majority of children and can become a writing lifeline for some.

> Since I have started teaching through drama, the children are enthusing about lessons instead of forgetting them. (D4LC action research primary teacher) (D4LC 2005)

> That drama lesson was the best I have seen in the last 5 years. Every child was engaged. (PGCE tutor and an ex primary headteacher) (D4LC 2005)

> The students (particularly the boys) improved dramatically during this drama unit of work. Some raised their national curriculum levels from 3 to 6 and all students made good progress. (Secondary drama teacher of 14-year-olds) (D4LC 2005)

Table 1.1 (page 12) shows some of the problems that can arise when children try to write.

Once a child has acquired a view of themselves as a 'less able' or 'below average' writer it easily becomes self-fulfilling, as well as personally and emotionally damaging. One of the

Table 1.1 Problems with writing can arise when children . . .

Don't have enough ideas or confidence to get started	*I just can't think what to write about. I don't even know what the first sentence is going to be yet.*
Start writing but then soon run out of enough ideas and can't sustain their writing	*I don't know what else to write now. I'm stuck so I will just write 'the end' or 'and then she woke up'.*
Need support and encouragement while they are writing	*Writing makes me worry but I will have a go if someone will help me.*
See themselves as failures at writing and so have disengaged	*I know I am no good at writing so why bother to try?*
Become fixated on getting the technical aspects right to the detriment of the content	*I can't write any more until I have got all the punctuation and spelling right so far.*
Stream out content with no pace and little attention (before, during or after) to organization and structure, punctuation and grammar and no willingness to edit or correct	*I was the first person to finish writing and I don't want to do any more with it. It's finished.*
Are risk averse and avoid experimenting as writers	*I wrote something last time and the teacher liked it, so I'll just write something like that again to be safe.*
Rely heavily on other people's ideas	*I like sitting with this group because some people in this group have got really good ideas for writing and I haven't, so I can use theirs.*
Focus on the handwriting rather than the content	*This is my very best handwriting. I like my writing to look nice and neat.*
Are given writing tasks that are not well matched to their skills level and interests	*This is too hard for me. I feel upset about this and I don't want to tell the teacher because she thinks I am good at writing.* *This writing is too easy for me. I'm bored and I can't be bothered with it. My teacher must think I'm useless at writing to give me this.*
Find sitting still and working at a desk for long periods difficult	*I get fidgety if I have to sit still for long. I just need to move for a while. I wish the teacher would let me write lying on the floor like I do at home.*

difficulties with an assessment-driven education system is that children soon know their writing level and if they are trying hard but their level is 'below average', this can be de-motivating and demoralizing, leading often to disaffection or even disruptive behaviour.

> My son tried really hard in the writing test. When he was told his writing level was a Level 3 not a Level 4, he got very upset and told me he was useless. He told me he had failed writing. In fact he was only a couple of marks off a Level 4. I told him he'd done really well (he is very dyslexic) and that he had not failed but he just got really angry and shouted at me and said, 'Everyone knows that Level 3 is a failure'. It was all very upsetting. (A mother and teacher) (Baldwin 1999)

Primitive behaviour can kick in when children feel anxious or exposed in school. Children who do not write well often feel exposed. In drama situations these children may feel less 'fear' (a response to threat) when working in a 'flock' (a group or whole class) and when they can get out of their seats (moving may make them feel less vulnerable). They have less need to 'fly' from the situation (escape to the toilets) or 'fight' (exhibit challenging behaviour).

When children are working in mixed ability groups together in drama on a related writing task, those who struggle to write alone can be supported by working with a 'flock' of peers. The focus appears to be on the drama rather than on the writing and on the group rather than the individual. This can be less personally threatening to children who need support. Drama can enable a less able writer to be socially and actively involved in the drama and collaboratively in the writing without being put individually and publicly on the spot as a writer. Drama (and writing collaboratively in drama) requires and enables genuine 'group work' requiring real group interaction and problem solving towards a shared goal.

Humans are social creatures and most feel the need to 'flock'. Focusing on improving their writing and working hard at school is often not congruent with being seen as 'cool' once children reach adolescence. The social side of life tends to take precedence and 'belonging' to a cool group is often seen as more important than achieving well. Drama is a social way of learning so holds a particular appeal, allowing learning while working socially with a group. There are children who thrive when writing in drama situations and wither when writing in traditional English lessons.

> A child who had been absent for most of the drama work but present for writing the sequel, had access to a planning map and words to help her. She used the key incidents on the sheet but didn't develop these or describe them like the children of similar ability present for the drama work did. (Primary drama teacher of 8-year-olds) (D4LC 2005)

Children can lack confidence and not perceive themselves as writers. In drama, a well-established strategy, 'Mantle of the Expert' (MoE) enables children to assume the role of professional writers or other 'experts' with writing responsibilities and a compelling need to complete a particular writing task. While using MoE as an approach, the children treat each other respectfully as if they were real experts and imagine themselves as having competencies that in reality, they are aspiring to. One of these competencies can be writing well. MoE can help build children's self belief and confidence as writers and the quality of their writing often improves as a result. A parallel might be that athletes 'up' their performance by imagining they are winning a race. Children can 'up' their writing performance by imagining they are great writers!

For example (Unit 6, Activities 3 and 4), the TiR as the Minister for Food, asks the children (as his expert advisers) to look at a draft official statement before it goes public and to suggest and justify possible amendments to it. These activities require and share 'writer talk'. The children need to read with a 'writerly eye' to consider how the public might respond to various parts of the statement (thus considering purpose and audience) and they need to communicate to the Minister of Food diplomatically and using 'writer in role' talk.

Poorly differentiated teaching and tasks can negatively influence writing performance. If a task is too challenging (or not challenging enough) and the support is insufficient (or too much) then a child can 'fail' in their own and others' eyes. The child may internalize this as their own failure, whereas one could argue that the 'failure' was the teacher's for not matching the task well enough to the child. This happens from time to time and is only really damaging if tasks set are consistently too hard (or too easy). In drama differentiation is often by outcome (although sometimes by task) but with shared responsibility among the group for that outcome. It is a supportive and collaborative forum for writing with the opportunity for children to contribute individually at their own level, to group success.

How can drama help us as writers?

We know that drama is:

→ highly motivating and enjoyable

→ stimulating and novel

→ social and collaborative

→ physical and kinaesthetic

→ emotional and empathetic

→ personally challenging

→ excitingly risky at times

→ different to other lessons (novelty)

→ inclusive and supportive

→ verbal and non-verbal.

Some brief examples have already been given as to how drama can help children as writers. Table 1.2 shows how drama can help address some common problems with writing.

Many of the common 'problems' and inhibitors that children experience as novice writers can be at least partly addressed through drama as a pretext and context for writing.

Drama gives moments of tension and time for vocabulary and ideas to incubate. Research by Cremlin et al. (2006) explored the types of support that drama offers primary school children as writers. The researchers found that the main features of drama that helped school children produce effective writing were:

→ the presence of tension

→ the degree of engagement

→ time for incubation

→ a strong sense of stance and purpose gained in part through role adoption.

> When all these connecting threads were evident in a drama and a moment for writing was seized, the case study children's writing was recognised to be consistently high in quality. (Cremlin et al. 2006)

Table 1.2 How drama helps address some common problems with writing

Problems with writing can arise when children . . .	Drama helps address this by . . .
Don't have enough ideas or confidence to get started	Supporting the generation of ideas collaboratively that are then shared and belong to the group
Start writing but then soon run out of enough ideas and can't sustain their writing	Providing a new focus or deepen a current focus, thus sustaining the children's interest and sustaining the fiction which is inspiring the writing
Need support and encouragement while they are writing	Enabling collaborative writing, with the children all supporting each other to complete the writing task/s for the drama
See themselves as failures at writing and so have disengaged	Giving collective responsibility for the writing, so that no individual child should see themselves as personally failing (especially as they are distanced through being in role)
Become fixated on getting the technical aspects right to the detriment of the content	Working collaboratively on all aspects, so a child fixated on any aspect would be moved on with the writing by his/her peers
Stream out content with no attention (before, during or after) to organization and structure, punctuation and grammar and no will to edit or correct	Enabling a flow of ideas from everyone that can be written at the time and returned to later for redrafting in groups or as a class
Are risk averse and avoid experimenting as writers	Encouraging a risk taking in the drama that can spill over into a risk taking attitude to writing in the drama
Rely heavily on other people's ideas	Enabling the sharing of ideas by groups of different sizes, as well as individual writing tasks if appropriate
Focus on the handwriting rather than the content	Enabling the content of the children's writing to deepen the drama or drive the drama forward
Are given writing tasks that are not well matched to their skills level and interests	Differentiation by outcome, with children having opportunity to work at their own level while contributing to shared and guided writing
Find sitting still and working at a desk for long periods difficult	Not only being active, visual, auditory and kinaesthetic but also with times for reflection and stillness

All the drama units in this book build and use dramatic tension to catch and keep the interest and attention of the children. They are whole drama lessons that need time for the deepening of children's engagement with the role and situations, time to incubate their ideas before what Cremlin et al. (2006) would call, 'seizing the moment to write'.

Just the quick use of a drama strategy or two in English lessons might slightly and immediately improve a piece of subsequent writing, for example by generating and sharing vocabulary and phrases together in an accessible way, but for deeper contextual understanding and more significant and sustained improvement, teachers will need to give time to the drama itself to support the children to achieve high quality writing through drama.

Drama provides contexts for writing

Drama is very flexible and can provide endless interesting and meaningful contexts for writing. A drama can be set anywhere, at any point in time or in any place, with any situation happening involving any character/s.

Rather than teachers presenting children with writing tasks that seem to have come from nowhere (except maybe a past test or exam which many associate with anxiety), the writing tasks that arise within a drama, are connected immediately with the children because they are already engaged with the drama they have helped create, before any writing task emerges from it. They are co-owners of the fiction and understand the context and need for the writing from an insider's perspective.

Instead of receiving a writing task and just being told to 'imagine' (which is difficult for many children and adults), drama actively supports children to imagine together and helps them bring the imaginary contexts to life in a range of ways that are both verbal and non-verbal. They are actively and emotionally engaged with the imaginary contexts from which the need to write arises or within which pieces of writing that they read, belong (Figure 1.3).

Figure 1.3 In drama children emotionally engage with imaginary contexts within which the pieces of writing belong

Drama provides purposes for writing

If we can't see the purpose of doing a piece of writing, then we are less likely to put much effort into it and it is less likely to be good. Why expect children to strongly engage with a piece of writing and persevere with it, if they can see no value or personal purpose for it and have no reason to care about it?

Drama has had a very motivating effect on reluctant writers. They enjoy writing more because they understand the context and the purpose of the writing. (Primary headteacher) (D4LC 2005)

Teachers can skilfully adjust the drama to generate a range of purposeful writing opportunities that feel 'real' to the participants who are engaged through working in role. The writing opportunities are not 'bolt on' as they are embedded purposefully in the drama or arise from it.

The writing we are introduced to as readers and role players in a drama may help us to get to know characters better. For example in 'The King's Daughters' (Unit 2), the different school reports of the princesses are designed to provide the children with insights into their different characters before the children engage with them in role. This in turn will help the children when they portray the characters themselves in the drama, or write for the different princesses as speech writers.

The teacher can ensure that the text types the drama requires are those the children most need to learn about and practise writing. If the children need to practise persuasive writing for example, then the teacher might steer the drama towards a persuasive letter. There is an example of this in Drama Unit 5, when the children have opportunity to write persuasively to the Mayor of Hamelin. The writing purpose is to get the Mayor to solve the problem with the rats. They will be able to draw on the rat incident experiences that they have already devised and enacted together in the drama. The children will not be struggling to imagine content, as they have already lived the situation together in role and now just need to focus on organizing and writing their persuasive letter. They have a clear sense of audience as the Mayor will come responsively to life as the TiR. If the children need to practice instructional writing then the same drama can require them to design a 'rat elimination device' and write a sequence of instructions explaining how to operate it. If they need to practice diary writing, the scenes they are involved in will have given them ample material for a personal diary entry. They can practise filling in information questionnaires in order to present 'factual' information to the council in Hamelin. They can become poets and write additional verses for the poem, based on scenes and events generated in the drama. Whatever type of writing the drama requires them to write, they will already have a good base to start from, provided by the drama they are living in role.

An imaginative teacher will see many potential reasons and opportunities for writing in any drama. They will probably focus on the most useful, necessary and inspiring. The children care about the drama and feel and see themselves as writing 'for the drama' rather than 'for the teacher' or writing for writing's sake. Both teacher and children know in reality that there is an underlying, veiled focus on the children writing but the children willingly go along with this because they want to keep the drama going and maybe influence it with their writing. The writing spotlight is on the drama rather than the child and so they feel less exposed as they write. The drama is acting as a kind of Trojan horse with the writing embedded within it.

Drama provides audiences for writing

Writing is nearly always intended to be read by someone in addition to the author. Think about the many and various types of writing you may already have encountered and read today (including this book). Maybe you have read text messages today, a cereal packet, a newspaper headline or article, a leaflet, a billboard, a postcard, emails, instructions, an advertisement, directions, a recipe, a website and so on. All these pieces of writing were created and written by someone with a clear purpose and audience in mind. In school too often, the children do not have any sense of a real audience for their writing (other than the teacher or examiner). Drama can provide a 'real' engaged and present, audience that is responsive in or out of role to their writing. The children and TiR, become the knowing, present and responsive audience for each others' writing.

At school age children probably do not have many real audiences that they would be naturally writing for. Practising writing tends to involve children carrying out a series of one off and disconnected pieces of writing which are clearly just exercises and which are unlikely to be compelling unless the teacher has found some way of emotionally engaging the class with them. Many schools are increasingly creating opportunities for children to write to real people, companies and organizations as audiences, for real purposes. This is good practice and motivating for children. It gives a real purpose to the writing and sets up the likelihood of a genuine response. However, realistically children can't always be writing to real people and also cover the wide range of writing types they need to learn and practise. Through working in role, drama can bring any audience alive, into physical being and enable the writer in role to meet and interact with the imagined 'real' audience of their writing. In drama, children can (in or out of role) interact and talk with the audience who has read or heard their writing. The children, as writers and players, are present in the drama, to witness a character's responses and the impact of whatever they have written. Drama can emotionally engage children with 'real' people as a 'real' audience for their writing. The writing experience and the writing of course is absolutely real, even though the pretext and context is realistic.

In drama children become the characters who can also become the 'writers in role'. Co-participants in the drama become the audience too for any writing produced in and by the drama. The children and teacher can respond as the writer's audience, from a position of knowledge acquired by being inside and helping create the same drama. In Unit 1 for example, the children will collectively have become one housekeeper (collective role) who needs to write a reference for a servant. Later they might hear their own writing read aloud when they witness an employer (TiR) reading the reference they have written (and so they become the responsive audience to the impact of their own writing). Another example would be if the children are in role as royal speechwriters, interviewing a princess, before embarking on writing a very important speech for her. The later audience for the speech will be the king (TiR). The children can be in the court scene later as audience and will hear the princess deliver their speech. This again gives them opportunity to become the writers and the audience to their own writing. They can evaluate the effectiveness and impact of their writing and its spoken delivery by a princess, as well as gauge the response of the king to it.

The children in role are making frequent cognitive and affective shifts between being an actor, reader, writer, speaker and audience. Being able to shift in this way actively, reflectively and responsively, is an important skill that benefits both writing and drama. In real life it is unlikely that children will need to write a speech for a princess but the real skills they use and develop doing this in the drama will continue to be of use to them. Their awareness of keeping the audience in mind as a writer will also remain. Improvements in writing gained in drama lessons need not be lost once the drama is over. The drama was pretend but the thinking, learning and improvement in writing is real and should remain with them.

Good drama builds up gradually, is sustained and connects the writing experiences and tasks. It offers a cohesive and sustained fiction within which writing is generated and belongs. It also offers an engaged, continuing and knowing audience, who remain present in different roles, responding with understanding and speed to that which is written. Writing in drama is usually carried out at the moment the drama requires it and gets an immediate response from the 'in role' drama participants as the audience for the writing. This audience includes the teacher. The writing enriches the drama experience and the drama experience enriches the writing, with both benefiting from and sustaining each other.

Drama provides motivations for writing

Young children who are developing normally, are highly motivated to spend considerable amounts of time role playing in their imagined worlds (alone and with others). The universal human need to imagine and pretend is neurologically driven (Baldwin 2004, 2012) and probably helps explain why children enjoy drama (Harland et al. 2000). From about the age of 2 onwards, they play, re-play, act and re-enact 'real life' and story experiences. This imaginary world activity may be increasingly shifting towards solitary engagement with electronic games in virtual worlds, to the detriment of physical and socially interactive activity (Dreyfus 2000).

In their natural, dramatic play young children voluntarily generate emergent writing, at times enjoying the physical activity and the feeling of imagined competency it gives them. They are getting ready to write and writing in drama later can be seen as a natural development of this.

Structured role play areas and activities usually have opportunities for mark making and emergent writing purposefully embedded within them, for example the pretend cafe may have a pad and pencils available in case children want to take orders from customers, or the children may have created the advertisements for the class shop, and so on. Hospital corners may have prescription pads, and travel agents might need children to 'write' with keyboards and screens as they try to find holidays for their pretend customers. If children feel motivated to write while dramatic playing, they have the materials ready and waiting.

> Young players are instinctive authors as they create their play worlds and we should be drawing on this experience rather than marginalising it . . . when children are offered facilities for writing within their play, they will often use them. (Hall and Robinson 2003)

Writing while engaged with others in an imagined experience is not something that needs to stop after the early years. In drama, we can offer the same. Good drama teachers see the potential for continuing to build on this through structured dramas with embedded writing opportunities (as exemplified by the units in this book). Pre-school dramatic players may have parents or carers who join in and support the children's writing in role activities and children in education may be fortunate to find drama teachers who will continue to do this at a higher level. For some children, a drama approach might make all the difference between success and failure at a writing task at any age.

Children enjoy 'pretending' and drama. Enjoyment is a key motivator. Once we enjoy something, we want to do it again and we gradually get better at it (whether it be drama or writing). Research on the effects and effectiveness of the arts in secondary schools (Harland et al. 2000) found that drama is the most motivational of all arts subjects. It is a very popular choice for pupils when they have access to it. If children find writing an enjoyable activity when it takes place within or after a drama lesson, then the enjoyment and writing are linked and this linking writing and enjoyment may extend beyond the drama lesson.

> It was good to see the children using reasoning and thinking skills during the session and some of their ideas were really surprising. After being in role children were asking to write! (Primary headteacher) (D4LC 2011)

Drama can make writing a supportive, social experience

Human brains are wired to be social. Children need to socialize, to become part of groups, to belong, to make sense of lived experience with and alongside other people. They spend a great deal of their lives in school, being told to sit still and listen to teachers, to work independently, not to copy, to do their homework alone, and yet we also want children to develop holistically as people with good communication and interpersonal skills. To achieve this they need to have time to be together, work together and talk together (Figure 1.4).

Drama is a way that children can learn together and drama can only work if they are interactive and cooperate and collaborate. Too often children talking and working together in school is seen as getting in the way of learning rather than it being considered as learning.

Figure 1.4 Children need time to work, talk and write together

It is enjoyable and socially appealing to work in groups with peers in a serious yet playful way with a clear learning focus. Maybe drama is popular with children specifically because it expects and encourages them to work and talk together, to solve problems and create characters, situations and narratives together. Drama and collective/collaborative writing both need the children to listen to each other, discuss, cooperate, negotiate, compromise, in order to be successful at the drama and/or the writing. Drama as a learning medium relies on the children using and developing their social skills because drama itself is a social activity.

> Collaborative arrangements in which pupils help each other with one or more aspects of their writing have a strong positive impact on the quality of their writing. (General Teaching Council for England: Research for Teachers 2008)

Children also need to be able to write alone as well as together. However, achieving shared success as a collaborative or collective writer (as in shared and guided writing) will nonetheless help children to develop their writing skills and give a feeling of success that may transfer when the child is writing alone later. Knowing that a piece of writing will be later used in a drama can be motivating for reluctant independent writers.

> All children wrote independently, including those children who had previously been quite resistant to writing. They worked with purpose and pace, wanting to reach the point where they could read it back in role. (A teacher action researcher) (D4LC 2005)

Whole-class drama creates its own collaborative community of 'role players' who can seamlessly move into becoming a community of actors/players, a community of writers or a collective audience for each others' writing.

There was a burgeoning of shared and guided writing activities that were introduced through national strategies. These sometimes involve children and teachers as co-writers, working collaboratively on writing tasks, talking aloud as writers about the process ('talk for writing' and 'writer talk'), working together towards a shared writing outcome. Drama fits perfectly with this more social and collaborative approach to developing writing. The TiR can work as model, scribe, collaborator and talk as a writer in role with the children as co-writers.

Writing with others can be stimulating and enjoyable, especially when you share imagined and emotionally compelling experiences in the drama from which to write. Instead of competing with their writing, the children are cooperating in order to help the drama advance. When the drama is progressing well, the children know that their writing has been an essential part of this. They can also reflect and rework their writing individually or together out of role later, when the drama lesson is over, reawakening their memories of the drama and re-evoking their emotional responses to continue the writing if necessary.

Drama can help build children's confidence and self-esteem as writers

Drama can help build confidence and improve children's attitudes to writing. This holds true for children of all ages and abilities (D4LC 2005) but for children who are particularly struggling with writing and those who have become disaffected by failure, drama can be a lifeline for re-engagement and for building up their self-esteem and belief in themselves as writers.

> Lower ability writers were more confident and more focused during writing lessons linked to the drama. They were keen to get their ideas from the drama, onto the paper. (Year 10 secondary school drama teacher) (D4LC 2005)

As drama is a social and collaborative activity, it requires the whole class (regardless of ability or disposition) to be involved or it can't work well, so peer pressure comes into play. Children who avoid writing or struggle with it are likely to become engaged nonetheless by drama as they don't want to be excluded by their peers (who probably want the drama to work). Also working supportively with collaborating peers, can leave children less individually and personally exposed, with the result that they may be less fearful about the writing they are doing together. The ideas of a less able or less confident writer can be valued, used and emerge within a successful, jointly owned piece of writing. They play their part in a successful piece of writing and success is a great motivator.

In many schools the educational diet children receive is rather repetitive, so children often enjoy drama because it is learning in a different way and has a novelty effect that can be capitalized on. If the drama is interesting they will stay interested and the positive effect on writing can be sustained.

> Empowering children to have the confidence to share their thoughts and ideas verbally (in drama) will then inevitably lead to the development of their confidence to commit their ideas to paper. (A teacher action researcher) (D4LC 2005)

The most competent writers in a class are not always the children with the most imaginative ideas and drama often reveals this. Sometimes classmates find themselves looking at each other anew when a child who has difficulty with the process of writing comes up with the best ideas and when a child who lacks confidence to write, works very confidently in role. Education too often notices, values, develops and uses only some of the skills that children bring with them.

> He had a negative self image and was difficult initially to engage in class . . . He began to engage with the drama sessions as they caught his imagination. And he was able to contribute his ideas and suggestions. As his ideas were being taken seriously by his peers (and by himself) he engaged more with the strategies and began to take ownership of the drama developments . . . his peers began to perceive him as a boy who had useful ideas and would help move the drama forward. (A teacher action researcher) (D4LC 2005)

In drama children are often playing the roles of adults who have status, responsibility and tasks to do (some of which may involve writing).

> Two children who are usually quite difficult to engage were particularly responsive to the drama approach. They showed increased motivation and interest and were empowered by the opportunity to talk and work in role. They had a stronger sense of self-esteem being addressed as police officers. (Year 5 teacher, Acle St Edmund Primary School)

As police officers these children might have reasons arising in the drama to take notes, compile a police report of an incident after talking with eye witnesses in role or maybe fill in an incident questionnaire. Police officers (and other professionals) may also have an unspoken personal viewpoint on issues and events that can emerge through confidential diary entries.

Drama generates ideas for writing

Writers draw on their real life experiences and their fertile imaginations to get inspiration for their writing. Most children obviously have had far fewer and narrower real life experiences than most adults and have less to draw on first hand experientially. Many children however, have fertile individual and collective imaginations if they are given the chance in school to use and develop them rather than curtail them. Writers are generally good at drawing on and transposing real life experiences into imagined experience, drawing their ideas from what they might have seen, heard, read or imagined and transposing them onto the page as text. This is also what children are doing together in drama to some extent. They bring their ideas to the drama (stimulated by first hand experiences or stories, films and their play), and they pool their ideas to help create and sustain a shared, imagined experience which can then be transposed into (or contain) writing.

Children will probably need to come across other people's ideas in order to inspire their own. Both reading and drama are among the important ways of getting access to the ideas of others. Children need time and opportunity to work playfully together in role with their own and other people's ideas and from this, new connections can be made and new ideas generated. The class is a drama community which provides an in role forum within which children's own ideas are listened to, where they can see their own collective, and other people's ideas take shape (sometimes literally through physical form). They are 'in the moment' and present as ideas are generated, selected, used, played with and developed within the drama that will also feed their writing.

> If you don't know what to write, drama helps you see other people's ideas and that gives you ideas. (Child, age 8, Aldborough Primary School) (D4LC 2005)

> When working in this way (drama), they add ideas to each others work and the ideas build up. This boosts their confidence and when we actually get to the writing stage they are brimming with ideas and confidence. (Special needs teacher of 11- and 12-year-olds, Mile Cross Middle School) (D4LC 2005)

As children grapple with what they might write in drama, and have and share ideas, they will also be explaining their thinking, justifying and arguing for choices about vocabulary, form, content and organization and so on. They will be learning from each other, with the teacher alongside them as a co-participant, and sometimes a co-writer at the very moment of writing.

Drama provides structure to support and develop the writing

Drama for learning and for writing is a highly structured activity. Teachers who avoid drama may be under the misapprehension that it is too loose an approach but the level of structure is in the hands of the teacher and the drama strategies available to a teacher are like a set of scaffolding, with each piece offering something different in terms of what it can support. Most good drama lessons are highly structured and focussed but also give opportunity for creative thinking and action.

In terms of developing narratives particularly, drama provides a very clear structure, as all drama is a story in itself. Once the children are inside the drama, they are also inside a story as collective storymakers and tellers and can then become storywriters and tellers, during or after the process.

> Drama helps me to make sense because I already know what is going to happen in my writing. (Child, age 9) (D4LC 2005)

During drama, reasons emerge or can be planted, for children needing to produce many types of non-narrative writing, for example, a persuasive letter or an eye witness incident report, graffiti, lists and so on. Again, teachers can pick from their strategy toolbox, whichever strategy most appropriately supports the writing type (see Chapter 2, Table 2.1). The structural support for writing in and through drama is not just on paper, it is a living, multi-sensory and often physical structure that is experienced and then recalled. The strategies are visual, auditory, kinaesthetic organizers that scaffold the children's thinking and speaking in advance of the writing, thus acting as memorable organizers prior to writing.

The various individual drama strategies and conventions themselves can all be seen as separate structures or as pieces of scaffolding that can be joined together in sequences. A drama strategy in an English lesson might be used in isolation, to help children to organize and maybe voice their thinking before writing or strategies can be used in carefully structured sequences to create drama lessons that are structurally more sophisticated and effective as a preparation for writing. Chapter 2 of this book analyses some sequences from the units in detail to explain how this works in practice. There is nothing to prevent teachers from stopping the drama from time to time, in order to directly teach (out of role), what is necessary for the writing but the more the drama can flow, the more easily the children sustain their cognitive and affective engagement with it and the deeper the experience is likely to be. It is possible sometimes for the teacher to teach directly for the writing from within their role, if the role is carefully selected. For example if the children were novice journalists and the teacher was in role as a trainer of journalists, then the teacher can teach about writing from within the role.

> The story of the drama could be made collaboratively, but a sound structure could be established to guide their writing. All the children could contribute and have their ideas incorporated into the main story. All parts they had to write were mentally and orally rehearsed easily without them saying 'I don't know what to write'. It could also be stopped at various points to teach or reinforce any literacy skills needed prior to writing. (D4LC action research teacher, 2005)

> The children find writing through drama work helpful. They find the medium more interesting and memorable and an aid to the creative process to have sorted it all out before they put pen to paper. (D4LC action research teacher, 2005)

Drama uses and develops the thinking skills necessary for writing

Drama can be seen as thought in action (or thought in the making) with an aesthetic form. Different types of writing are underpinned by the need to employ different types of thinking. Drama can be used directly to stimulate and develop different types of thinking that underpin different types of writing.

→ Drama stimulates, requires and supports individual thinking and inter-thinking.

→ Drama shares and presents inter-thinking in visual, aural, kinaesthetic and tactile forms.

→ Drama stimulates and demands different types of thinking and inter-thinking from its audience (who may also be its participants).

The various drama strategies and conventions (see Drama Strategies, pp. 50–61) can act as both thinking frames and writing frames and can be linked directly to the development of different types of writing (see Chapter 2). If a teacher is clear about the type of writing that he wants the children to develop, then he can select a drama strategy that will support the type of thinking that underpins that particular type of writing. Good teachers, who are practised in using various strategies, might decide to adapt them to try to make them fit even more directly with their specific learning and writing objectives. Teachers can change and bend strategies towards different writing purposes and types of writing as exemplified in the drama units, parts of which are analysed in Chapter 2. They can choose strategies to specifically get the children to engage in different types of thinking, prior to producing different types of writing (Table 1.3).

Table 1.3 How different thinking skills are developed through drama

Type/s of thinking	Example/s
Focus their attention on particular moments or characters or events.	Through the use of still image (focus on a moment) or hot-seating (focus on a character) or a devised scene (focus on an event).
Retrieve and bring to consciousness from short- and long-term memory past information of relevance to the drama task for further processing. Retrieval may be multi-sensory.	Through creating and engaging with a role that is based on past, real experiences and memory.
Formulate questions and enquire.	When questioning characters through hot-seating. Through the use of statement prompts, such as, 'I wonder . . .'
Gather and/or generate information of relevance to the drama or writing task.	Through reading in role or through improvisation or through the use of 'role on the wall'.
Encode and store information through a range of drama forms, visually, auditorily, kinaesthetically and tactilely.	Through devising scenes that have information within them that can be performed repeatedly.
Organize and arrange information so that it can be better understood, used and communicated to self and others in aesthetic and/or written form.	Through devising scenes or still images that communicate significant information and meaning about the characters or plot.

Type/s of thinking	Example/s
Sequencing events episodically.	Presenting a series of still images or scenes that convey episodes in the drama.
Transposing the form but not the substance of information retrieved, acquired or created.	When presenting a character first realistically in a scene and then symbolically as a role sculpture or vice versa.
Identifying and analysing parts and the whole.	Recognizing key moments or scenes in the drama and their impact on characters, plots and outcomes immediately and over time.
Recognizing relationships and inter-relationships and patterns of behaviour and/or threads running through a drama (or story) and seeing how they relate to each other.	Through 'forum theatre', which often focuses on changing negative patterns of behaviour.
Identifying main ideas, reasons, characters, motives, events, messages, themes.	When retelling the drama through a series of key images with captions and/or minimal speech.
Recognizing inconsistencies.	When participating in 'collective role' and portraying a single character there is a need to ensure that the character's speech and/or behaviour is consistent.
Generating new ideas and new meanings.	Through improvisation and working in role.
Delineating fact and inference.	When deciding (and possibly recording through 'role on the wall') 'what we know' about a character and 'what we think we know' about them.
Anticipating next actions, events, episodes and outcomes.	When devising short scenes or still images that portray possible alternative endings.
Elaborating.	Through returning to scenes that have already taken place and adding to, or extending them (possibly through improvisation or scriptwriting).
Connecting and combining information.	Bringing a range of ideas together to be presented as one image (e.g. as a 'role sculpture'). Or gathering individual responses to a moment in the drama, as single sentences and then arranging them into a collective poem. Or gathering information together around a 'role on the wall'.
Restructuring to accommodate new knowledge and information.	When improvising and working in role, accommodating new information received from others in role and adapting, assimilating and integrating it seamlessly into the ongoing improvisation.
Assessing and evaluating the quality of ideas and **selecting** from them.	When devising a short scene as a group and only using ideas offered by some of the group's members.

Drama helps children acquire, use and apply knowledge needed by writers

It is likely that schools that use drama as a context for inspiring and developing writing use this as one approach and that they may also use others. No single approach is the answer for all children. It is interesting to look at a variety of approaches and materials that schools already use for the teaching of writing and consider them through a possible, whole-class drama lens.

For example the 'Talk for Writing' approach that many primary schools use (developed by Pie Corbett), has strong links with active storytelling. Its core is the use of re-enactment linked to communal, oral storytelling using specific gestures linked to particular words and phrases. The approach reinforces story content and structure by linking them to associated movements and embedding them through repetition, gradually moving on to children taking more ownership of the story through elaborating or using their own language to tell it. They will also perform and re-enact the known stories before moving on to create their own. Having embedded the stories, children can be encouraged to work creatively with them and maybe whole-class drama could be a good way to develop these stories and help the children take increasing ownership of them. Writing opportunities can then be embedded within the subsequent whole class, creative drama process.

A lesson created by a teacher in the 'Drama for Learning' (D4LC 2005) school improvement initiative used a Pie Corbett version of the story of 'The Three Billy Goats Gruff' in which the Troll was protecting the field from the goats because it had rare orchids in and the Troll in this drama was not up to the task! Through whole-class drama and using the children's in role ideas, they improvised a scene in which they put the Troll through the equivalent of performance management interview and listed the aspects of his job he needed to improve at, for example, 'Be fiercer'. These 8-year-old children ended up creating a different job for the Troll, selling plants outside a school where he could get free reading and writing lessons, as the Troll (TiR) could not read or write! Writing opportunities emerged for a poster to keep goats off the bridge, a new job description and an advertisement for a new bridge Troll and a letter of thanks from the old Troll who was learning to write but had his first ever letter scribed for him by a group of children.

Most teachers have a stock of well loved stories that have become embedded in their teaching that can be re-viewed through a drama lens and brought creatively to life to further benefit children's creativity and writing.

2 How Drama Strategies Support Writing

What are drama strategies?

Drama strategies are established techniques and forms that drama teachers should know and have in their toolbox. Active teaching and learning strategies (see pages 50–61) should surely be of interest to every teacher. They are flexible structures that can be acquired, used and adapted for a multiplicity of drama, learning and writing purposes (as well as for any learning across the curriculum). They can be focused and tailored to specifically introduce and develop compelling pretexts and contexts for writing in role, while simultaneously developing an engaging and worthwhile drama. Drama strategies offer both a structure and a form which can hook children's interest and help prepare them for writing, as well as support them during the writing process. The strategies can also be seen as aesthetic building blocks for developing the drama itself. The drama units in this book employ a wide range of drama strategies and conventions that exemplify how drama can inspire and support children to write well.

A few drama strategies are already commonly used in many English lessons (often overused). These include hot-seating, freeze frame, thought-tracking and conscience alley. However there are many less well-known strategies and variations of the commonly used strategies that are being continuously and creatively evolved and developed by innovative, playful, reflective practitioners.

How to set up and carry through a drama strategy, is not set in stone. Teachers can and should be able to be creative, innovative and experimental, adapting strategies in ways that may best suit their learning and teaching purposes and their classes. They will need of course, to be evaluative and reflective about the impact of what they do and the outcomes. A skilled drama practitioner will consider what they need for the children to learn, practise, achieve, explore or understand next and which strategy might be the most effective for this.

The role of the teacher

TiR is arguably the most important and powerful drama strategy of all. It brings the teacher and children together in a unique way that is truly interactive, at the moment of learning and writing. Both teacher and children are simultaneously engaged with the drama but also safely distanced from it by being in role. Good whole-class drama is done *with* the children and not just *to* them, or *for* them. The TiR is a co-participant, an enabler, mediator, support, guide, provocateur and is pivotal in helping ensure the drama works for the children and for the learning and writing purposes.

In role the teacher can help the children to imagine a shift in status positions and instead of the teacher always being the one with the knowledge, skills and the power in the classroom, together with a class they can agree to suspend disbelief by maybe helping the needy TiR. The children can be sharing and using their imagined (and real) knowledge and skills from an imagined, higher status position (such as when using TiR but with the children as the experts).

TiR can be used:

→ to give information;

→ to gather information;

→ to stimulate, inspire, provoke and/or challenge thinking, speaking, emotion and/or action;

→ to organize and ensure focus and structure;

→ to model and guide children as 'players' and writers;

→ to support and affirm the children's contributions and share ownership of the drama.

Specifically in relation to drama for writing, TiR can be used:

→ to set up a compelling, imagined context that children need to write within;

→ to introduce compelling, imaginary (yet seemingly authentic) purposes for writing;

→ to be a responsive audience for the children's writing;

→ to guide and share writing in role, offering support, encouragement and focused praise to the children during the writing process;

→ to act as a co-writer, modelling thinking aloud and 'writerly talk' in role;

→ to focus and pace the writing process as a co-writer;

→ to introduce different types of writing (as a character) at appropriate moments within the drama;

Figure 2.1 Teacher in role can be pivotal to both the drama and writing

→ to place the teacher's own writing within the drama itself;

→ to scribe if required;

→ to link and mediate between the drama and the writing experience.

What follows later in this chapter is an analysis of sections from each of the drama units contained in this book. Several sections of TiR are analysed because it is so pivotal in relation to both the drama and the writing that can be inspired by it (Figure 2.1).

What do drama strategies actually do?

Drama strategies can help children organize, and give visual form and voice to their thinking and inter-thinking, through engaging children both cognitively and affectively, prior to and during the writing process. Drama strategies can not only act as aesthetic forms and structures but also as pre-writing, writing and post-writing evaluation activities.

Thinking and speaking and creating drama are all closely linked and can be integrated. When taking children through drama, on a writing pathway, teachers will need to consider, which types of writing are supported most appropriately by the various drama strategies, before and during the writing process. It is worth considering the type of thinking and speaking necessary to prepare children for writing tasks of different types and then select the drama strategy that will help develop this.

Table 2.1 gives some brief examples of how some specific drama strategies can support writing.

Table 2.1 How individual strategies can support writing

Strategy (for definitions, see Drama Strategies, pp. 50–61)	An example of how it can support writing
Role on the wall	This helps children record briefly and visually, notes about an individual character and their characteristics. Over time several can be collected to record a character's development. These can act as a sequence of writing frames. Role on the wall can be used to collect any sort of predefined information about a character, for example, facts, opinion, thoughts, speech fragments, actions, motives, emotions and so on.
Teacher in Role (TiR)	This brings a character to life, enables verbal and non-verbal interaction with the character and can generate dialogue that could then be scripted. TiR helps children to get to know aspects of a character first hand and with the teacher deciding what to say or hold back. A TiR can help drive a narrative forward or focus the attention of the children where it is required for the drama (and maybe for subsequent writing). A TiR can also use the role to feed in or gather information, build tension or add complications into the drama plot (as a writer does in a story or novel).
Collective role	This lets children in role collaboratively contribute to the creation of one character and their speech. It helps children feel closer to the character.

Strategy (for definitions, see Drama Strategies, pp. 50–61)	An example of how it can support writing
Role sculpture	This raises the children's awareness of the multifaceted composition of a character. It helps children when writing in role later as that character or when creating and understanding scenes with the character in.
Conscience alley	This enables children to see a character's dilemma from polarized viewpoints. They listen and contribute in turn, to reasoned argument, which can help prepare them for persuasive writing.
Freeze-frame	When a scene is frozen at a key moment, it enables investigation and interpretation by participants and audience. The scene's significance can be reflected on individually and collectively. Discussion in and around the image will provide ideas and vocabulary that can be used later for writing.
Still image (devised)	A still image is planned and devised by the participants. In order to plan for maximum impact they need to synthesize what they are trying to depict visually and communicate it clearly. These thinking processes are also central to the writing process.
Image theatre	This usually involves devising contrasting images, depicting the reality and the ideal of a situation in the eyes of a character. To create both images authentically and collaboratively the children need to come to a shared understanding of the current situation and how it could ideally look in the future, as well as what a character is trying to achieve. Once there are still images they can be brought alive and become the source of action and dialogue that can then become script or prose for example.
Storyboard	This is a series of images. If they are created after the drama, they can act as a narrative writing frame. Thought and/or speech bubbles, captions or more extended explanatory and/or descriptive text can be added.
Captions	When images have been created, they can be given a one sentence caption that can be written and placed with the image (rather like a picture in an art gallery has a title that synthesizes what the picture is about).
Essence machine	This involves the class in performing relevant sounds and actions repeatedly that link to a theme or a moment in the drama. This focuses their attention on significant auditory moments, actions and gestures, some of which they may give prominence to in subsequent writing that draws on the multi-sensory.
Hot-seating	This involves asking a character questions that they answer in role. It often gives opportunity for note-taking leading to reporting. It can provide factual information to the children that will help them better understand a character that may feature in subsequent writing of various types. Or, if they are asked to write as that character they will be better able to do so.
Talking objects	Children become objects of significance to the drama (or to a character in the drama) and are able to speak individually or to each other. This activity not only deepens their understanding of aspects of the drama and its characters but also can pave the way for writing that involves personification.
Eavesdropping	The teacher passes scenes that the children have prepared or improvised and pretends to be eavesdropping unseen. Only the group scene (or the part of the class scene) being eavesdropped is active. The rest wait still and silent. If the scenes are sequenced it can help focus the children on episodes that can be the structural basis of different paragraphs or chapters.

Strategy (for definitions, see Drama Strategies, pp. 50–61)	An example of how it can support writing
Eye witness	A group or class scene is prepared or improvised and shown. The audience become eye witnesses to the scenes. This can become the pretext for writing eye witness accounts. It is possible for the whole class to be in role and then come out of role and write as eye witnesses to the scene they were actually involved in.
Thought-tracking	Listening to the inner thoughts of characters can offer the material for writing a soliloquy.
Teacher narration	The teacher can act as a narrative storyteller, telling the drama back to the children in narrative form. They hear their collective drama as a story and this heard structure can support them later when writing stories.
Active storytelling	This embeds the structure and content of a story through the physical re-enactment of it. The teacher may tell the story and the children act it as it is heard. When the children have used their bodies to act out the story, it aids recall of it later when they write it.
Statement prompts	This involves everyone having the opportunity to completing sentence openings verbally that are usually focussed by the teacher. For example, the focus can be sensory, 'I can hear . . .' or emotional, 'I am feeling . . .' or can encourage enquiry, 'I wonder . . .' and so on. They can be written on sentence strips and arranged as a collective poem.
Choral speaking	This requires all children to closely engage with the same text. It enables the director/s (which can be the children collectively) to draw out the particular emphasis and significance of certain key words and phrases through performance.
Soundscape	This involves the class in making an improvised or prepared performance of just the sounds, relevant to a theme or a moment in the drama. This focuses their attention on only the auditory aspects of a scene which may then give prominence to in subsequent writing.
Voice collage	This involves the class in making an improvised or prepared performance of just selected key words and short phrases from the drama. Words might be repeated, overlapped, and so on, for maximum meaning and impact. The voice collage may be unravelled and words and phrases are given further prominence in subsequent writing.
Mime	Acting out a story (or part of a story) without words, will evoke a response in an audience that can lead to inviting the audience to add the words. This may be through speech or just describing or telling the narrative.
Mantle of the Expert (MoE)	Children in role take on the responsibilities of workers (often professionals) with specific tasks to do, usually for an imagined external client. These tasks can be professional writing tasks, reports, design briefs, legal documents, posters and so on. MoE easily provides a pretext for writing non-fiction texts.
Mapping and drawing in role	If children map the place where the drama takes place then this can provide a shared visual reference point for creating and describing settings visually (adding to the map), orally (talking in role about the map) and then through writing the setting later. Maps can also have written labels and keys. When children are asked to draw in role as a character, it can reveal much about a character. It can also help children to organize their thoughts visually before writing with their drawing available for reference.

Strategy (for definitions, see Drama Strategies, pp. 50–61)	An example of how it can support writing
Devising and performing	This is self-explanatory. The children create a short original piece of drama together (maybe just a short scene) with the intention of performing it to others (usually this is a group work and the rest of the class is the audience). The process results in a product that can provide the content for various types of writing, for example a critical and evaluative review of the performance, scripting the performance.
Forum theatre	This involves creating a short scene or series of scenes by consensus around an authentic situation that needs remedying for a character or characters within the scene. After seeing the performance once through, the audience can make suggestions to the characters about changes they then try out through improvisation. Or the audience member can take over from the role from the actor and show the change/s he wants. Forum Theatre generates many alternative endings to scenes. The improvised scenes can then have the different endings scripted. The situations depicted may give rise to relevant writing opportunities, for example the characters in the scenes may keep diaries or write graffiti or leave letters to be found, and so on.

Although isolated strategies can be very useful as a way of bringing an engaging drama activity into a lesson (English and other subjects) to support writing specifically, it is when teachers are able to create strong sequences that help create and sustain an ongoing and compelling drama, that they can achieve so much more for writing and for drama.

Examples of how drama strategies work together to support writing

What follows are sections taken from each of the drama units in this book, highlighting the contexts, within which various strategies are used and how they achieve both focus and flow in ways that support writing through a whole, sustained drama. The analyses take account of what the children have already experienced and practised in the lesson/s, prior to a specific strategy being used and explain the way that the children's thinking, speaking and listening is being focused 'in role' as they move towards producing writing of different types. The sections from the units have been selected to cover together a wide range of drama strategies in context and a range of different types of writing tasks and types.

Mary Maguire (Drama Unit 1 on pp. 67–75)
Statement prompts ('I wonder') (Unit 1, Activity 2 on p. 68)

The children have heard the poem and may have read it themselves. In Activity 1 they are invited to think about what Mary as a housemaid in Victorian times might feel. Empathy with the main character is being encouraged and supported.

The 'I wonder' statement prompt activity is then introduced and focuses the children's thinking towards enquiry. They speak aloud in role, what they are wondering about Mary (which may involve hypothesizing). The rule is that they must all start their single statement aloud with the same opening, which on this occasion is, 'I wonder . . .' . The rule offers a clear, safe and ritualistic structure for the children to make and share their short verbal contributions. Listening to each others' 'I wonder' ideas may then spark new ones, as well as the children having gained ideas from each other.

'I wonder' focuses children on open-ended, rhetorical questioning, stimulates curiosity and helps lead to shared enquiries that may be answered by the evolving drama. The teacher might decide to offer the first statement prompt herself, to model an opening statement if she considers that the children need this. Alternatively, the teacher may hold back from contributing a statement and avoid being a model, if she considers it would be more beneficial for the specific class. The collective 'I wonder' statements let the teacher know where the children's interests lie and at the same time (towards writing) it provides the basic material for compiling a collective poem of the statements, which the children write on sentence strips. Everyone can contribute their one statement to one collective poem in which all the lines will all start with 'I wonder'. This means it will immediately hang together cohesively in terms of structure as each line starts with the same two words. The verbal in role 'wonderings' are written and then transposed from one art form to another (from drama to poetry).

When the children together are negotiating and agreeing the sequencing of the sentences of the poem, the process requires them to justify, explain and give logical reasons to each other, for the exact placement and sequencing of the various lines in their collective poem.

The opportunity to then read or perform their collective poem (which was arrived at through drama), enables them to move straight into performance poetry, merging the arts forms of poetry and drama.

Image theatre (Unit 1, Activity 9 on p. 71)

In small groups, the children create two still images. One image depicts the way that the housekeeper wants the servant (Mary) to behave ('ideal' behaviour). The second image shows how the children think the servant is feeling inside ('reality'). The two images can be juxtaposed to clarify the difference between the reality and the ideal, that is, the difference between how Mary behaves and how she feels. This activity gives opportunity for the children to empathize, as they are needing to think about the characters' feelings and inner thoughts and this can draw them into empathy. They are trying to 'get inside the head' of the character, and this draws their attention to Mary's inner conflict.

The images created (through discussion and negotiation within the group) will present the ideal and reality in an aesthetic form and encourage analysis and reflective thinking. The teacher may decide that the creation of these images should be done with, or without speech. These two different approaches lead to different types of thinking and talk and both approaches could be tried. Making an image without speech and talking about it afterwards leads to reflective, retrospective explanation, remembering, justification, evaluation and analysis of what led to the finished image. Talking about the image as it is being created is likely to lead to speech containing more direction and instruction.

There is then a script writing opportunity suggested for a scene between the 'two Marys' that could lead to previously improvised or prepared dialogue being turned into a short, written playscript. Their playscripts could then become the basis of a short performance. The children could be given opportunity to direct their own or each others' playscripts for performance, which gives a real purpose to their scriptwriting and makes clear and brings alive, the essential links between writing playscripts, directing performance and influencing audience. Passing your playscript to someone else to direct means there is a real need to be clear with regard to directions. This playscript will have been written once they have already gained a deeper understanding of the character through the previous still image making activity.

The use of contrasting still images ('the reality' and 'the ideal') links closely to the practise developed by Augusto Boal (Brazilian theatre director and writer) who worked with 'Image Theatre' with the aim of effecting personal and social change (Boal 2002).

Reading in role/Teacher in Role (Unit 1, Activities 13 and 14 on p. 73)

The children have been introduced to different types of writing (within the drama) that include a job reference written for Mary, extracts from her diary and Arthur's letter (Writing Resources 5, 7 and 8 on pp. 156, 158–9). Each different type of writing is written from different characters' viewpoints and for different purposes. The children need to read these three different pieces of writing in order to deepen their engagement with and knowledge and understanding of the characters, so that they can join in the drama appropriately. Drama provides the reason they need to read the writing analytically and evaluate it. The children also hear the pieces of writing read aloud in role (so will get a stronger sense of the different writing types and the character when the pieces are performed aloud and in effect become scripts). The clear writing models they have been presented with (the 'Writing Resources'), can also be used as writing frames in the future if required in lessons other than drama. Each different piece of writing they have read (or heard) in role gives more information about the main character and her life (from different perspectives) and is likely to make the children increasingly curious.

Meeting the character Arthur (TiR) is held back in this unit plan until after they have spent some time as 'Text Detectives' and so meet Arthur with some opinions and questions to ask. They are being drawn into a dramatic enquiry that requires them to read, focus, analyse text and subtext, evaluate, hypothesize and postulate, and enquire in role. They are likely to be curious and keen to get information from Arthur for the drama. What they learn from the TiR as Arthur will not only feed the drama but also the character appraisal that may be written afterwards. Being told they will be able to interview Arthur (through hot-seating him) builds anticipation (dramatic tension) and becomes the pretext for them writing and gathering their list of questions first, which are then put to Arthur (TiR) live. The children interview Arthur (not realizing that they may be gathering information needed to write a character appraisal later). The children's thinking, reading, speaking, listening and then writing have all been stimulated and integrated by the drama and will underpin the writing that may follow.

The teacher is guided towards improvising Arthur's role in a balanced way. This makes his character more interesting and believable and is likely to keep the children intrigued. Arthur comes across as a mixture, a real, thinking, feeling person and not simply a goody or baddy with transparent motives. This keeps them wondering. Arthur is a puzzle and the TiR is intended to divide their opinion of him. This makes the task of writing of a character appraisal more challenging than if Arthur was just being presented as a stereotypical character.

The King's Daughters (Drama Unit 2 on pp. 76–86)
Teacher in Role/Mantle of the Expert (Unit 2, Activity 9b on pp. 80–1)

The children, in role as members of the King's Inner Chamber, have already been called by letter to a secret meeting. This letter has been received, read and responded to in role. At the meeting (as members of the Inner Chamber) the children read the school reports of the three princesses (analysing these information texts for insights into the characteristics of the different daughters). Reading reports as advisers, will fuel possible concerns and the prediction of possible problems that could arise if the King goes ahead with his intention to divide up his kingdom. When talking with the King (or offering him their written advice), their professional role as wise courtiers will require them to them to speak (or write) formally and to be circumspect and diplomatic.

Thought-tracking is then introduced to free them to speak their innermost 'in role' thoughts aloud. Still in role as members of the Inner Chamber they are then given the opportunity to speak to each other as pairs in role (giving opportunity for less guarded speech and for hypothesizing and predicting). This is after the thought-tracking and so many inner thoughts signalling concern, have been voiced for all to hear. The children have used or heard highly guarded and formal speech when talking with the TiR as King, and generated and gathered supposition and rumour when speaking slightly less guardedly to a trusted colleague (in pairs). The drama strategy 'eavesdropping' is then employed as a way of enabling the less guarded speech to now be heard by all. Listening to the inner thoughts and the eavesdropped concerns will have built the dramatic tension and given the children ideas to use in their writing. They can now shift roles from Inner Chamber members to newspaper reporters and use the ideas that they generated through working collectively in role, for newspaper report writing. What they write is likely to be a mixture of fact, rumour and supposition, as this is what the drama has generated so far. They have acquired the information they need from the TiR as King (information giving) and through the reflective and collective thought-tracking process, as well as from each other when talking as pairs of advisers who were eavesdropped. They will now be recalling and then selecting from what they created together, synthesizing information and probably sensationalizing it into a newspaper column. They have the information and ideas they need and are likely to still be highly engaged with the drama, when they are creating a newspaper report that may be shared with the class afterwards, as a knowing and responsive audience.

Role on the wall (Unit 2, Activity 13 on p. 82)

This is a well-established writing (jotting) activity used to capture and record key aspects of a character around a drawn outline of that character. This might be on paper or the whiteboard for example. The jottings (maybe written on self-adhesive labels that can be moved around or on word/sentence strips) can be written individually first or collectively at the time of writing (depending on what the teacher thinks is of most benefit to the children and the learning) but the jottings should be shared. The 'role on the wall' can be used to capture a character's traits, thoughts, speech, actions, or their feelings or indeed anything worth recording about a character at any time. It is a visual organizer and written record that is then available throughout the drama and may be added to and referred back to as the drama develops and we learn more about the characters as events unfold and more is revealed.

In Unit 2, following on from the scene where the three sisters have just met with their father, King Lear and been told he intends to divide up the kingdom according to their declared love for him, 'role on the wall' is being used to gather and record the different feelings and responses of the three princesses (using three separate roles on the wall). What is recorded while carrying out Unit 2 will have been arrived at through textual analysis and through 'in role' activity. What is then gathered on the wall about each character can then be used as the basis of writing interior monologues and/or character appraisals.

In Unit 2, Activity 14, the jottings will be written on three different coloured sentence strips (one colour representing each character). Sentence strip content was on this occasion, confined to the emotional responses of the princesses on hearing of the king's intentions. The children's collective, 'in role' responses that are gathered and organized through role on the wall, can become next, the basis of poetry, which can then be performed (thus merging writing and drama). The different types of writing have their own dramatic purpose and are responded to by a knowing and responsive audience (the class itself, including the teacher). The children's cohesive, collective writing belongs to them and to the drama and is being continuously inspired and fed by it.

Teacher in Role/collective role (Unit 2, Activity 14 on p. 82)

The children are all collectively in one of three character groups as one of the three princesses (either Goneril, Regan or Cordelia). Through collective role they will be all sharing responsibility for an important character's improvised speech and will need to listen to each other carefully, so that they are convincing as one character. First however, the children read the diary extracts (Writing Resource 4 on p. 162) which they are told have been written by the princesses. They need to read them purposefully, analytically and evaluatively in order to carry out their role-playing with authenticity. They are likely to listen well to the other people playing the role collectively with them, as they will probably not want to let their group down. They will need to work consensually and listen actively, to keep track of how other members of their character group are responding, what they are exactly saying in role. If they don't listen carefully they will be likely to say something inappropriate or inconsistent with the character group they are in. They will be playing the scene depicted in the diary entries, so need to read them carefully before devising and dramatizing the scene they have read as a diary entry by a princess.

Earlier the children read the princesses' termly school reports (Writing Resource 1 on p. 160), which revealed aspects of their characters. They are gradually, actively exploring and building up the characters of the princesses now. They have a drama purpose for reading and analysing different types of writing about or by the princesses before collectively improvising as a princess.

The diary extracts (Writing Resource 4 on p. 162) are all personal recounts by the different princesses of the same key scene (when their father says he will divide up his kingdom). Together in collective role the class all recreate and enter this scene as if they are one of the three princesses. They need to speak and respond from three different viewpoints (and have added to 'role on the wall' to help prepare them). Once they have become part of a particular princess through the 'collective role' strategy and talked in role as the princess, they are likely to have emotionally engaged with (and be able to represent) their particular character's viewpoint and portray authentically their known characteristics. They may also have gained more information about the daughters from the king himself (TiR). The 'collective role' activity provides a good basis for moving the children then into some collaborative writing in role. They could for example, write tomorrow's speech now for their particular princess.

The children have gained information and insight, while in role as princesses (collectively) but then are asked to shift roles and status, when challenged to write graffiti as commoners. The scene they have engaged with as princesses, has provided them with the information they need to now write politically driven 'One Nation' graffiti (a form of social commentary) as the common people. In the drama they feel the excitement and tension associated with the writing graffiti, as its illegality is stressed. Graffiti requires the children to synthesize, as this writing form requires a minimum of words written for maximum emotional and political impact on the reader.

The Year of the Rats (Drama Unit 3 on pp. 87–96)
Performance carousel (Unit 3, Activity 9 on p. 90)

Having read or listened to Writing Resource 1 on p. 166 being read (which is a piece of prose that describes an imaginary row of fine shops in 'The Grand Parade' in Hamelin), small groups of children choose one of the shops and create a pair of still images, depicting two contrasting scenes in that shop. The first scene is before the rats infest the shops and the other is after. This focuses their attention on collaboratively negotiating and creating visual representations of what is depicted within Writing Resource 1. It also helps the children to engage with a specific place and incident.

Performance carousel is then used to enable each group in turn to present their still images seamlessly, so that the scenes are quickly melded into a collective performance piece which contains all the still images they have created in groups. Using performance carousel aesthetically is an improvement on the teacher just asking each group in turn to show their images. They are all immediately placed in the same continuous performance without the drama mode being broken until the carousel is over. The children have devised scenes and are performing while present in the performance carousel; they are simultaneously audience and co-participants. Through watching each others' scenes, they will have gained more information about what is happening in 'The Grand Parade' since the arrival of the rats. The knowledge they have acquired will be of help if/when they fill in the formal questionnaire (Writing Resource 3 on p. 169) and/

or to complete an 'Audience Response Report'. Individual group's scenes can be evaluated hopefully with focused discussion prior to the children starting to write. It is suggested that they focus their 'Audience Response Report' on three things they liked about another group's images and one thing they think could be improved.

In this unit, the images presented through performance carousel are still and silent but a performance carousel can also involve presenting short scenes with sound and/or speech. This can support the scripting of scenes. Scenes can also be presented with an accompanying narrative spoken by the teacher or one that simply links the scenes. Sometimes an appropriate musical soundtrack in the background helps blend the scenes into one performance. Seeing many scenes and/or images can be a helpful pre-stage to the children writing their own narrative prose about a scene or scenes.

Teacher in Role (Unit 3, Activity 14 on p. 91)

The TiR as the cynical and provocative Mayor of Hamelin is dealing with angry townsfolk who are victims of rat infestation and attacks. The children know there is a problem because they have read it as a story, heard it as a poem and have lived it in role, creating and performing scenes in rat infested shops. They became eye witnesses to the vermin while watching each others' scenes. The TiR as Mayor feigns disbelief, to provoke indignation and encourage reasoned argument and vocal protest from the children. The public meeting can provide an opportunity for formal minutes to be taken (possibly by a group of children in role, taking notes as clerks). The 'clerks' might just be asked to each record one or two significant exchanges at the meeting. This can be done using a writing frame (Writing Resource 4 on p. 170) and/or the teacher could show them a real set of minutes as a model. Filming and playback of the meeting could help this minute writing process.

It would also be possible to have a group of newspaper reporters taking notes at the same meeting. Comparing the notes of the clerks and the newspaper reporters could be worthwhile. Do they pay attention to the same things, write similar notes but end up writing from them very differently or is the note taking itself different because their writing purpose is different? Differentiated writing tasks can arise from the same scene. The Mayor (TiR) could give a press conference for the children as newspaper reporters, so that they are actively asking questions of the Mayor and not just eye witnesses recording a meeting. Or the children could create an official press release for the Mayor. The drama units contain suggested writing activities but they can be adapted, substituted or added to by teachers to best match their particular children's needs and abilities.

Mantle of the Expert (Unit 3, Activity 15 on p. 92)

What Hamelin needs is someone with rat catching expertise and the drama strategy, MoE is used to give the children the responsibility of being rat catching design experts. They have already read the advertisement (Writing Resource 5 on p. 171) and in role, are responding to a professional design brief, which will involve them in a professional writing task. They are led to imagine and feel they have the knowledge, skills and understanding of expert rat catchers. Their task is to design a 'rat elimination device' and 'pitch it' in writing to the Mayor and present it in only a minute. The time limit prevents this from being a long writing task and ensures that the main selling points of their inventions are the focus. They collaboratively generate design and presentation ideas, prioritize, select, synthesize, justify and sequence, before completing the short writing task. If there was time, their 'expert' presentations could be synthesized as short PowerPoint presentations (thus integrating ICT). Alternatively the writing activity could be extended, for example by telling the children that although they will only have 1 minute to present their group's designs to the Mayor, they can leave supporting materials (maybe a brochure) for him to look at later.

A less challenging task for some children could be for them to present their design pictorially but with annotations and labels. This can act as a prompt sheet when they present verbally to the Mayor (TiR). The role empowers the children and helps them feel they are confident and competent designers whose expert skills are needed. Enjoying this feeling, they are likely to wish to sustain in through the writing task, rising to the role of the writing challenge, while protected and supported by being in role with others and with the teacher available to guide and support.

A pre-design or further enquiry activity could involve the children gathering 'rat facts', maybe accessing information and making notes from appropriate internet sites about rats. This will help build their credibility as experts and may influence their rat elimination device designs. They could be asked to research, list and present, ten true and surprising facts about rats to impressively present to the Mayor! Experts could be challenged to find the most amazing 'rat fact' that will help them in role to try to out-do each other when they present to the Mayor.

Conscience alley/conscience forest (Unit 3, Activity 25 on p. 95)

The class in role are asked to individually decide whether the piper should be paid, now that the rats have gone. They physically represent their positions and viewpoints, by dividing into two lines or groups (pay and don't pay). This creates an alleyway between them for the TiR as Mayor. As the Mayor passes by, each child has opportunity to briefly explain and justify aloud, their position on this matter as the townsfolk. This can lead into a writing activity with the children writing the 'for' or 'against' arguments heard (as well as their own), on individual paper strips. The arguments on the paper strips can then be prioritized by moving them into some order. These sequenced sentence strips can become a persuasive writing frame for individual, shared or guided writing. Access to both sets of arguments can provide material for writing a reasoned and balanced argument.

The children could also be asked to draft a letter from the Mayor to the piper, stating and explaining the Mayor's decision. They are empowered to do this confidently, as they have rehearsed the content through drama and are clear about the purpose and audience.

The Lost Bag (Drama Unit 4 on pp. 97–107)
Teacher narration (Unit 4, Activity 4 on p. 99)

The children have contributed already to creating a collective, pictorial village map (contributing to building the imaginary setting for the drama and engaging with it). They have given themselves an appropriate role and selected, focussed on and described aloud one particular place in the village that has personal and emotional significance for them (their favourite place). While doing this the children have been speaking ritualistically in role. It is at this point in Unit 4 that teacher narration is used. The teacher can use Writing Resource 2 on p. 174 (narrative extracts) but it is suggested that the teacher should also weave in additional information and ideas that have come from the children through their mapping and talking in role thus far. The children's collective ideas and descriptions become the threads of a sustained narrative, spoken aloud by the teacher and woven into the fabric of the drama. The teacher speaks almost as if he is storytelling, or as if reading aloud the descriptive, opening setting of a book. The teacher uses the children's ideas as the source material, signalling that their ideas have been listened to and are valued and that their ideas can become part of a compelling narrative. They hear a familiar setting that they have contributed to visually and orally, becoming a seamless story opening. The teacher's modelling of narrative talk supports the children to hear their ideas in a narrative before moving into their own narrative writing, which the narrative speech has prepared them for.

Working in role (Unit 4, Activity 8 on p. 101)

The teacher is in role as a representative of the Ministry of Information (an intermediary role with high status). He 'in role' has introduced an instruction leaflet to the children (Writing Resource 4 on p. 176), which they have read and discussed in role as villagers. The teacher deliberately withholds information and only partially answers the villagers' questions to arouse their curiosity and concern. The official then withdraws, leaving the children chatting together as concerned villagers who have many still unanswered questions in their minds. With the children in a state of individual and collectively heightened curiosity, they are led by the teacher straight into a writing in role activity and are asked to write the questions that they wish they had asked the representative from the Ministry of Information. Sharing their unanswered questions collectively (and recording them in writing) is likely to further stimulate their curiosity as they will feed off each others' questions. As the questions have been recorded, they can return to them at other points in the drama to see if they have arrived at any answers as the drama has progressed.

Ritual (Unit 4, Activity 21 on p. 106)

The class have attended a meeting as villagers, which leads to a dramatically tense opportunity to write covertly in role to a tight deadline. The children find covert writing exciting. Their letters will be smuggled under cover of darkness to the outside world to an audience of their choice, for example, the newspapers or a friend. Attendance at the meeting will have built the tension, supported emotional engagement and given the children (as villagers) content for their letters, which are written in role. A ritual is then introduced that involves an envelope and it provides a visual focus. The writers each select from their letters and share aloud chosen, significant fragments of their writing. Each writer in turn puts their chosen fragment (written on a sentence strip) symbolically, into the same envelope as his fellow villagers. This ritual is serious and compelling. The various written and spoken sentences, when collected, voiced and ritually placed in the one envelope, are given symbolic significance and the collective ritual also unites the children in their covert endeavour. Each child's sentence contributes to an unrehearsed and meaningful, short performance.

This way of sharing writing in role through ritual, creates a serious mood, tension and drama. It is infinitely more dramatic and interesting than going around the whole class and listening to everyone reading their whole letter out (which would take too long and possibly become boring). It is also practical and gives everyone a brief but significant opportunity to speak. It also gives each child control over the sentence they decide to select, contribute and perform. Drama again has provided a stimulus for writing in role, and the writing produced has then become the stimulus for further drama.

Lorry (Drama Unit 5 on pp. 108–17)
'Move if . . .' (Unit 5, Activity 1 on p. 109)

This strategy can be used to open any drama. The teacher invites each person to consider whether various statements apply to them personally and whenever a statement applies personally, the children signal this by moving to another part of the circle. The statements are all linked in some way to the themes of the drama which they are about to enter. 'Move if' is used as the opening activity in Unit 5 and it leads into note taking and writing a short report. 'Move if' does not always have to lead into writing.

After Unit 5, Activity 1, there is a suggested activity in pairs. One child is interviewed by the other (and can then swop over). The task is to interview a partner about one of the statements that applies to them personally and elicit their real life experience in relation to this. The child being interviewed can select the experience they are willing to be interviewed on. This gives a pretext for interviewing someone about a real experience in their lives, note taking and then writing a short report from the notes taken (as reporters do). This activity will have led participants into recollecting and recounting situations and incidents from the past that will be of direct relevance to deepening their personal engagement with the ensuing drama. The report writing is only given 10 minutes. This links with the speed that real reporters sometimes work at and also it means that the children can swiftly move back to building the drama.

Still images (statues) (Unit 5, Activities 2 and 3 on p. 110)

The progression between Activities 2 and 3 links closely with Boal's (2002) 'Image Theatre', which often conveys and contrasts 'the ideal' situation and 'the reality' as still images. On this occasion the images the children make together are statues. They have been introduced to 'the ideal' through the image of the Statue of Liberty and a poem about it by Emma Lazarus. The symbolic statue and short poem welcomes immigrants to a new life. So the children have engaged with the drama theme through image and poetry before interpreting and transposing the poem into further images through drama. They are interpreting and creating through several art forms, sculpture, poetry and drama.

A contrasting sign from Arizona (dated 2010) is then introduced. This warns people to keep away from an area of 'human smuggling'. The children again interpret this using several artforms. The Arizona sign is used as source material for devising a contrasting statue which is the modern day antithesis of the Statue of Liberty. The children then express the meaning conveyed by their statue, as poetry (as Emma Lazarus had done with the Statue of Liberty). Using drama they have created 'the reality' as a statue in Arizona (stimulated by the written sign in Arizona) before transposing it again as poetry. Reading, writing, speaking, listening, devising, sculpting all interflow and stimulate each other. Drama, as a visual, auditory and kinaesthetic art form has helped support the flow between art forms. The additional word level support has been provided by asking the children to select key words at various points in the process, to help them focus and synthesize their thoughts before embarking on poetry writing.

Choral reading (Drama Unit 5, Activity 9 on p. 112)

Using thought-tracking (Activity 7), the children have spoken aloud in role and shared with each other their reasons for leaving their imagined homelands. Each child completed the statement prompt, 'I'm leaving tomorrow because . . .', before being asked to write their letters in role, on the eve of their departure. They have mentally rehearsed and spoken aloud their reasons for leaving before they start trying to elaborate and explain them in writing. The thought-tracking supports the letter writing in role, and helps the children engage more deeply with their character and theme. Their letters have an immediate and responsive audience, when they are placed in an exhibition (Activity 8), which the children all pass through as engaged readers, noting significant phrases and information.

In small groups the children then return to re-read their own letters and each selects a sentence and writes it on a sentence strip. This involves them in weighing up the relative importance of sentences they have written (selecting and prioritizing). In groups of six, their collective sentences now become the collective source material for creating a group choral reading performance. This immediately gives shared ownership of the choral speaking to the children, as all will have contributed a significant sentence from their letter to the choral performance. They have to engage with each others' writing in order to successfully devise the group choral performance. During the process of devising the choral reading, they will discuss, and experiment with words, sounds, effects, volume, repetition, echoes, and so on, to highlight meaning and have maximum effect on an audience. Each child will experience a sentence of their writing valued and becoming part of an integral part of a collective performance. The drama has led to them writing and then selecting from the writing, in order to create poetry and performance together. Reading, writing (sentences, letters, poetry), speaking and listening in role, devising, performing and responding are all integrated, supporting and feeding each other.

When the Bees Died (Drama Unit 6 on pp. 118–29)
Teacher in Role (Unit 5, Activity 3 on p. 120)

The Minister for Food (TiR) has a high status position in the drama but needs help with rewriting an important message for the people. The children's thinking, speaking and listening and writing as advisers to the Minister is valued and the children in role are being given high 'writing expert' status by him (thus raising their confidence and self-esteem). The TiR is setting high expectations of the children as skilled writers.

Writing Resource 2 is a draft statement from the ministry that the children are asked to improve. The audience is the general public and the purpose of the statement is to keep the public calm. Every word is important and the children need to take on a professional and political responsibility in role, to consider and predict the possible impact of various words and phrases in relation to the public's response as audience of the writing. Unrest needs to be avoided. Writing Resource 2 gives the children the same starting point and writing frame to work with and helps the children engage more deeply with complex issues central to the drama. As advisers to and writers for the Minister of Food, they need to read the given text analytically and in depth, review, edit and redraft collaboratively, all the time, predicting the possible impact of their writing on their imagined audience (the general public). The children in role will be both emotionally and cognitively engaged as they work collaboratively with each other and with the Minister. They know that their writing is important to the drama and will influence the final published public statement that will be released to the media.

Improvisation (Unit 6, Activity 7 on p. 121)

Children usually find it much easier to write playscripts if they have generated them through improvisation, rather than start to write from no active experience.

Having 'thought-tracked' in role as family members, the children in family groups improvise a domestic scene, showing how their family life might be affected by the food crisis as a result of the bees dying. The use of improvisation when devising performances can be a strategy moving towards a devised theatre performance. Improvised scenes can be refined and rehearsed if they are to become performances. The improvisations can also be used (as they are here) as the basis of scriptwriting. In drama we might start from a written script and improvise towards performance but here the children are improvising and then transposing this lived experience collaboratively into a written script. This helps them to understand that playscripts are rooted in drama and are not just a reading and writing activity. The written script may replicate or refine the speech that was generated though improvisation. The children can be selective about what they lift from the improvisation and will not necessarily need to record it all.

They are familiar with the characters, setting, plot and dialogue and the act of scriptwriting in this unit becomes about negotiating the writing with the group and making sure it is presented in playscript form. Once a group has written its playscript, it can become one scene among a series that form a collective, episodic play. The groups' scripts can be performed by the group or maybe given to other groups to perform and respond to as actors. If the group performing the script is to be different from the group that wrote it, then there is a real imperative to make directions clear. The speaking, listening, devising has preceded the writing and reading this time but the process in nonetheless integrated meaningfully and purposefully and has flow.

Soundscape (Unit 5, Activity 13 on p. 123)

The soundscape at this point in the drama serves several purposes. It is a way of dealing with a public demonstration without any physical risk. The use of a drumbeat defines the pace and provides structure and control. It also helps build dramatic tension.

The children as protestors enter with placards they have created through 'drawing in role'. However, the drama then moves the children to consider the sound of the protest (but without the visual and physical elements) by asking them to portray the scene as if it was in a radio play. By focusing on sound they will be considering and recreating the same scene through one sense and this will be for a different audience. The soundscape performance leads into a writing activity, through the suggestion that there would have been eye witnesses to this demonstration, who can write an account of the event. The children have built up to the scene as placard writers, lived the scene as demonstrators, considered the scene as onlookers and eye witnesses, before being asked to write (with a heightened awareness of sound as well as the visual elements of the demonstration). Again, the drama has provided plenty of content for the children to select from. They have recent visual, aural and kinaesthetic experiences to remember and draw on as they write, so their focus will be on selection, organization and form in relation to what they have experienced and witnessed.

Invisible (Drama Unit 7 on pp. 130–9)
Writing in role (Unit 7, Activity 7 on p. 132)

Many of the activities in the units involve writing in role in conjunction with other drama strategies that lead towards writing in role. This is a better starting point than expecting children to write in role when they have not actually been involved in any drama (as is too often the case) and have had nothing 'live' to do with the character.

In the above drama unit, the children have engaged with the characters through reading Ben's diary entry and analysing and interpreting its subtext. They have considered what they know and still wonder about with regard to the relationship between Ben and his mother. The children start to engage with the characters still more directly, when they then use Ben's diary as source material for creating still images that portray their understanding of the relationship between Ben and his mother.

Having discussed the mother/son relationship and portrayed it through still image, they now move into reflecting it in writing. The 'writing in role' task involves writing messages that Ben has received from his often absent mum. In the drama they are significant enough for Ben to keep them in a box and they are piling up! The children are invited to each produce two messages that Ben has received from his mum. In writing these the children will be demonstrating their understanding of this mother/son relationship, as well as contributing to the Writing Resource bank that is supporting the development of the drama itself. To write in role accurately and with authenticity, they must first understand the inter-relationship of the main characters. The children will enjoy writing fairly short, yet meaningful messages that others in the drama will understand and appreciate the significance of.

Performance (Unit 7, Activity 9 on p. 132)

Whole-class drama generates devised performances (often by groups) that are created and shared with and among the participants. Activity 9 asks the children to create a vocal performance, based on a sound collage.

Whatever type of performance children devise within drama lessons, there is opportunity for the audience (the class) to critically evaluate and respond to the performance. Being able to fairly and constructively evaluate a performance (as theatre critics do) involves a range of thinking skills but it also requires drama knowledge and experience.

The suggested writing activities are differentiated. One offers prompts to guide them when evaluating aspects of the performances they have seen. The other writing task suggested is more challenging and the children are asked to do a comparative criticism of two performances. Between these two activities would be the task of writing a critical evaluation of one of the performances.

Whole-class drama gives a regular opportunity for the written evaluation of the performances within it (which hopefully will be discussed prior to any written evaluation task). Teachers do not need to wait until there is a theatre trip or recorded performance to ask the children to write as theatre critics. The children's own drama is full of opportunity for evaluating each others' performances with the added benefit that it helps them improve their drama. As the children who are writing the evaluations of the performances, are also co-participants in the same overall drama, they are in a strong and insightful position to write authoritatively and with confidence about the performances they and their peers have devised.

Talking objects (Unit 7, Activity 13 on p. 135)

If children can talk with and become animate objects that belong to a character or who have familiarity with a character, then they can quite quickly gather a great deal of significant information about a character. As objects that can speak and that know a character, the children can contribute to building and developing that character and this can add an interesting and highly engaging dimension. Children as objects can be placed in an imaginary setting. Objects can offer a variety of information, perspectives and viewpoints about a character. First person speech by an object clearly supports children to understand and write using personification.

During Activity 10, the class have hot-seated Ben's mum (TiR) and then through two collective roles in Activity 11, they have been interactively in role, either as Ben or as his mum. In Activity 12 the class all become Ben's mum and are questioned by the TiR (a 'shadowy role' rather than a specific questioner role). So, by the time the children start to create and become the objects in Ben's bedroom, they are likely to be interested in the two characters and have a good understanding of them and the tensions in their relationship. It is at this point they become and/or talk to objects in Ben's bedroom to gather further information. The objects are not specified in the lesson but could for example include a football (worn), his bed (that knows his dreams), the box that contains written messages from his mum and so on. The teacher might decide to enter as an object him/herself. An object could be a piece of writing hidden or evident in Ben's room, which could give rise to additional writing opportunities, for example Ben's diary, his school report, a message he wrote to his mum but did not let her see, a text message to a friend and so on.

Having generated information as 'talking objects' the next activity in the unit (Activity 14) is 'role on the wall' which is used to gather and record information about a character. Having been in role as Ben, interacted with him, visited his bedroom and spoken with the objects there, asked questions about him and gathered and jotted what they know about him collectively through 'role on the wall', the children have emotionally engaged with Ben and been prepared by the drama for writing a character sketch. The drama is a strong support for all the children but for some it is a necessity that they experience the character 'live' before they can get started confidently on a character sketch.

Once They Get Started (Drama Unit 8 on pp. 140–8)
Forum theatre (Unit 8, Activity 10 on p. 143)

Bullying is clearly a form of oppression and the use of forum theatre in Unit 8 therefore is very appropriate. The children as spectators here support and/or advise the victim (TiR) how to try to move forward in dealing with the problem and what steps to take to start to break free of the oppressors.

In Unit 8, the children have already read a diary entry written by the victim of persistent bullying. The drama has required them to read and consider the victim's diary entry (which is likely to trigger personal recall and emotional engagement with the victim). Reading the diary helps the children gain knowledge and understanding of the victim's situation, actions, reactions and feelings. The diary reveals that the victim is having difficulty telling an adult that he is being bullied. In pairs the children have talked in role as onlookers (and eavesdropped others). By the time the Forum Theatre is introduced in this unit the children will have created and gained a fairly broad understanding of what the victim has been dealing with.

Forum Theatre is used here as a way of setting up and shaping a shared scene to help the victim tell someone he is being bullied. The children as audience (spectactors) are trying to empower the victim, so that he is able to tell an adult of his plight. Through the forum the children are advising and supporting the victim to take action and will be giving instructions and modelling through drama, how he might do this. Forum Theatre enables the scene to be played repeatedly and experimentally in different ways and enables the class to consider together, the most effective way for the victim to tell an adult about being bullied. The teacher here is acting as an intermediary between the evolving scene and the children as advisers and directors. As the scene keeps being re-improvised and is 'live' disclosure may take time to achieve and the responses of the participants are happening live and cannot be predicted. This makes the activity highly engaging.

Through the forum the class have been involved in analysing, creating, witnessing, evaluating, advising, directing, interrogating, supporting and reflecting as 'spectactors' (Boal 2002). Having exercised a range of thinking skills during the Forum Theatre, the children are well placed to start the subsequent diary writing task in role. Before the children write the new diary entry, they will already have studied the victim's previous diary entry (Writing Resource 6 on p. 202). They will be familiar with his diary writing style and have a model of it. They have witnessed in their minds and discussed in pairs some of the incidents the victim has been subjected to. They have listened in on others (through eavesdropping). They have actively engaged with the victim through the forum theatre and know first hand the turmoil and difficulties the victim in the drama is experiencing. This is a very strong starting point for writing the next diary entry as they have actively engaged both affectively and cognitively with the situation and the victim in a range of ways.

Drawing in role (Unit 8, Activity 11 on p. 144)

During Activity 9, the children had discussed (in pairs) a range of different bullying incidents that they imagined they had eye witnessed. These were then shared through eavesdropping. They are now invited to recall these, and synthesise them visually and symbolically as graffiti without words. This leads to a collective wall of graffiti being assembled that potentially becomes the source material for them to write a brief radio news report, describing the graffiti which has appeared. When they are asked to look at the wall of graffiti and then write as 'eye witness' radio journalists, they will be genuinely interpreting afresh the graffiti work of others.

Drama, speaking, listening, reading and writing, as well as symbolic drawing (visual imagery) have all been integrated with flow.

Writing and designing in role (Unit 8, Activity 18 on p. 147)

The children shift into role as members of the Anti-Bullying Intervention Team (MoE). They have therefore had a reason to read (in role) their professional guidelines (Writing Resource 4 on p. 200) and the TiR is the head of the team (high status role). This will help guide their actions and improvised dialogue when they are acting as anti-bullying experts called in by a school. The children have been given professional responsibilities and their job guidelines will influence their interventions and performances as well as the associated professional writing task they may undertake later.

At various points in the drama they have already actively created images and scenes of bullying and experienced them visually, aurally and kinaesthetically. While working their attention has been drawn in various ways to verbal and non-verbal body language in the scenes and to the effect of the relative positioning of the characters (proxemics) and they have been working with images both realistically (still images) and symbolically (graffiti).

By the time the children as groups of four 'experts' are asked to design an anti-bullying poster, they have been well prepared for this, having focused already through the drama on language and image and their juxtaposition for effect. When collaboratively designing the poster they will also be drawing on their collective, 'expert' knowledge to agree a high impact image and text for the poster. They may also be using and sharing their personal memories of bullying, as well as their new found knowledge and understanding gained through the drama.

The children are told the poster they design (as professionals) is for display in schools and is intended to appeal to a specific age range and must have a clear anti-bullying message with high impact. This gives them as designers, a clear brief with a clear purpose and target audience. Of course it is likely that these posters will end up being displayed in their own school and this will provide later a real as well as an imagined audience. Their posters could have a real, positive impact on tackling bullying in their own school.

Why not write what you need?

Teachers can spend a lot of time scouring books and the internet for different types of suitable writing to use in their teaching of writing and/or for drama. Teachers often are good writers and may find it quicker, more enjoyable and more effective to create what writing they need for some of their lessons. This can help ensure a really close match between the writing, the drama and the learning intentions of the lessons (as exemplified in these units). Also, if the teacher tells the children she has written the resource herself, this brings teachers as writers into the consciousness of children and helps them to realize that 'writers' are not some rare and distant species that have no direct connection with them. We are all writers.

It seems unfortunate that some teachers expect children to write but without engaging with writing personally themselves, either out of school or in front of the children. In role as co-writers, teachers can offer strong support and guidance to children before, during and after the moment of writing. In drama lessons or English lessons that use drama, the teacher can be in role as a writer and as a character and this can be highly engaging and inspiring. It can also greatly influence the content and quality of the children's subsequent writing.

As co-writers in role and co-actors, teachers will engage with the multiplicity of challenges and emotions that are involved in the writing process and in the sharing of writing. Working in role also helps teachers develop close, social, positive working relationships with the children they teach. Maybe this different teacher/pupil relationship develops because everyone is working so closely, meaningfully and interactively together with such a clearly shared and united drama and writing purpose. They create products together (drama and writing) that they can justly feel a shared pride in. Maybe drama works because it brings teachers and children together as players (in role) on common ground (the imaginary world).

3 Drama Strategies

Meeting and becoming people

Collective role

In a collective role several people simultaneously take on a single role. A collective role could involve two people, a small group or a whole class. The strategy allows shared ownership of a role and requires shared responsibility for making it work. Classes coming to collective roles for the first time might find the following guidelines helpful:

→ Always refer to yourself as 'I' and 'me' not 'we' and 'us'.

→ Even though you are in a group try to imagine that there is only one of you present.

→ Sit or stand close to the other members of the collective role.

→ Try to share the talking opportunities. As teacher you can impose a rule that no member of the collective can make two consecutive contributions. You can also help to distribute participation by aiming questions and comments at individual members of the collective or giving an object that is passed around and setting a rule that only the person holding the object speaks.

Role on the wall

This strategy enables a class to collate and display what is known about a character at particular points in the drama. Normally a drawn outline of the character is displayed and participants in the drama are invited to write things that are known about the character on adhesive labels. When stuck around the outline, the labels provide an audit of shared information. Different coloured labels can be used to record 'things we know' (referential) 'things **we think** we know' (inferential) and 'things **we'd like** to know' (inquisitorial) (Figure 3.1).

Role sculpture

Role sculpture is a way of allowing members of a whole class or a smaller group to contribute to a collective role-building and to deepen their understanding of a role. Having encountered a character in a drama, individual members of a group come into a central space one by one and freeze in a still shape which embodies something about the character. Piece by piece the sculpture emerges until the whole group has joined it. Digital photographs taken from different angles enable all participants to observe, discuss and evaluate the finished sculpture (Figure 3.2).

Figure 3.1 Role on the wall

Figure 3.2 Role sculpture

Teacher in Role

Teacher in Role (TiR) involves the teacher entering the drama by taking on a role alongside the children. This can be the most important and effective strategy available to a drama teacher. TiRs can be of high status (giving instructions, imparting information, setting challenges to be met or problems to be solved) or of lower status (asking for help, seeking advice or following instructions). Before taking on a TiR a teacher needs to:

→ Know the function of the role (e.g. to inform, to advance the story, to find out what the children have understood, to build tension, to present a challenge).

→ Decide how to clearly sign the role so that the children will know exactly who the TiR is supposed to be, for example, 'so when I sit down in this chair (or put on this hat or come through that door) I will become . . .'.

→ Ensure that the pupils know exactly who they are going to be while the teacher is in role. Are they also taking on roles or are they interacting with the TiR as themselves?

→ Adopt a commitment to the role. Brilliant acting is not required but a seriousness of purpose will make the TiR 'live' for the children.

Making decisions and judgements

Conscience alley (or decision alley)

This strategy in which members of a class literally take sides is very useful for reviewing an argument, sharing conflicting viewpoints public and taking stock of the factors which need to be considered before making a decision. The class divides into two groups depending on which side of an argument they or their roles prefer. The two groups line up facing each other forming a corridor or alley. A character with a decision or judgement to make can now walk down that alley. As he passes, each person in the line says something to persuade the decision-maker of a particular point of view. The person who travels down the alley will simultaneously hear opposing views or advice expressed and at the end of the journey can make a decision or judgement by joining one of the two lines. It is as if the character is hearing conflicting voices in their heads. This can be repeated several times with different members of the class experiencing the alley and reaching their own decisions.

Voting with your feet

This is similar to, 'Where do you stand' but here people place themselves on a line. The feelings of a group about a particular issue in a drama can be quickly and effectively gauged by indicating or drawing a line on the floor using string, chalk or a long paper strip. At either ends of the line two contrasting arguments or position statements are written on large sheets of paper. The class is now invited to take up a position on that line relating to their particular viewpoint. Stress that although some people may feel very strongly about the issue and feel the need to be at the end of the line others may be less certain and find themselves moving towards the middle ground. Having listened to the thinking behind these decisions using statement prompts to justify and explain, such as 'I'm standing here because. . .' you could ask if anyone wants to change position on the line. The activity can be repeated at various points in the drama. It is interesting to see if people change their positions having participated in the drama.

Where do you stand?

This strategy helps us to sympathize and empathize with characters in a drama. At any moment in a drama the class can be invited to show how they feel about a character by placing themselves in a space in relation to that character. If for example a king has made a decision you might ask people to stand close to the king if they think the king is right, or far from away him if they think he is making a mistake. In the case of an argument between two roles people can show which side they support by moving closer to one of the two roles. Statement prompts such as 'I am standing here because. . . .' can help to explain and justify the reasoning behind the person's positioning.

Making images

Essence machines

Essence machines can be made by small groups or by a whole class. The machine which can capture the essence of a moment in a drama, a character's feelings or a difficult decision is normally composed of three elements – movement, speech and sound. Members of the group become part of the machine one by one bringing with them a repeating sound, movement or fragment of language. Essence machines can be an effective way of examining contrasts. Machines can be 'operated' by teacher using signals which control volume and tempo. They can build up to include the whole class at the same time, or alternatively people (the machine parts) may enter or go from the machine.

Freeze-frame

A freeze-frame is the deliberate halting or freezing of action within a drama. The freeze needs to be cued for example by teacher calling out 'freeze', a drum beat or by the cutting of accompanying music. The freeze is an opportunity for members of a class to see and reflect on what is happening in the drama at that exact moment and perhaps to examine other people's frames together for interpretation, discussion and analysis. Just as a cueing mechanism is used to freeze action another cue is needed to reactivate it.

Image theatre

This involves the composition of a series of two or more still images. Often these images are contrasting showing different sides of an issue or a character, or may be 'the reality' of a situation in contrast to 'the ideal'. In image theatre slow-motion transitions between contrasting images can often make effective, engaging and meaningful performance to which words or sounds can be added.

Still image

A still image is also a moment frozen in time but this image has been devised and composed intentionally to represent an idea or moment in order to show it to others. Still images can be made by individuals, small groups or by whole groups. Although they are often composed using just participants' bodies, props, costumes and captions can be added to communicate additional meaning. Still images can be composed spontaneously and very quickly or built up gradually person by person. The image composition process can be accompanied by detailed discussion and verbal negotiation but it is sometimes interesting to ask groups to make their images without talking thus relying on non-verbal means of communication (Figure 3.3).

Figure 3.3 Still image

Storyboard

Storyboard is a form of image theatre which focuses on sequencing a narrative. Small groups may be asked to represent a story or part of a story by making a series of still images. In creating their images groups will need to think about character and incident but also about structure and sequence. For example some stories need to be told in chronological order but others benefit from flashbacks or leaps into the future. Transitions between the still images can animate the storyboard and retell the story while captions and speech bubbles can add commentary and dialogue. Sometimes a whole class can create a storyboard with subgroups taking responsibility for an individual part of the story. Digital photography and filming can provide one way of recording and sharing storyboards.

Still images, freeze-frames and storyboards can be given written captions. Although it could be argued that a well-composed image should be able to communicate its meaning without the need for words. However the writing of captions can sometimes encourage groups to reflect on their images from an audience perspective and perhaps to make improvements.

Asking questions

Hot-seating

Hot-seating enables us to find out information about people who we meet in drama but may also offer an opportunity to challenge and even confront characters. Normally the character to be 'hot-seated' sits in a chair in role and is questioned by the rest of the class who may or may not be in role themselves. The hot-seated role might be represented by an individual member of the class, a group undertaking a collective role or by a TiR.

Talking objects

In this strategy members of the class physically represent objects which can talk and interact. Some members of the class place themselves in turn, as objects in a specific location and other members of the class can then question those objects in order to find out more about a location, situation or character. When introducing the strategy for the first time it's important to stress that we are very interested in the object's perspective on the room in which it lives and the person who owns it. The physical representation is of secondary importance to what the object says. For example in Unit 1 a mirror on the wall in Mary Maguire's attic bedroom would be able to tell us if she takes a pride in her appearance but we would know nothing of her life outside the room. It is often useful to give people an opportunity to think of the questions they are going to ask an object before they actually 'meet' it.

Tracking thoughts

Eavesdropping (overheard conversations)

This is a way to access what is being said and thought by individuals, working pairs and small groups. It gives opportunity for spoken fragments to be heard by all. Short scenes are improvised for a while and then the action is frozen. The teacher walks around the space pausing in front of individual groups or pairs (as if listening in). This is a cue for a scene to reactivate (either moving forward or returning to replay what has already been said). We can 'eavesdrop' until the teacher moves on at which point the scene will freeze and the next will come alive and be heard as the teacher arrives.

Statement prompts

Statement prompts are useful thinking and speaking frames which offer a ritualistic, structured and supportive way for participants in a drama to contribute and share their ideas. In this strategy teacher provides the opening words of a statement which needs to be completed in turn by individual members of the class. Teachers can make up their own statement prompts. Statement prompts used in the drama units in this book include:

> **Unit 1:** 'I wonder . . .'
> **Unit 2:** 'I remember . . .'
> **Unit 3:** 'The first thing I saw was . . .'
> **Unit 5:** 'I'm leaving tomorrow because . . .'

Thought-tracking

This is the most frequently used method of accessing and sharing the thoughts of characters in a drama. At a given moment, a drama can be paused and everyone in role speaks the thoughts of a character, which might be their own character in the drama or else a designated character at that particular moment.

Thought-tracking: human keyboard

This is particularly useful in tracking the thoughts of collective roles. Ask members of a collective role to stand closely together and sum up what they are thinking or feeling in a word or phrase. Activate the chosen words and phrases by tapping group members on their shoulders. When tapped, each person will speak their chosen words. Shoulders now become keys on a keyboard. Interesting effects and meanings can be achieved by repeating the same 'note' for emphasis or playing two notes at the same time for synchronicity or contrast. Invite members of other collectives to play the keyboard. Experiment with two players (four hands) or three players (six hands). Alternatively invite the 'keyboards' to improvise without hands activating the 'keys' allowing people to decide for themselves the most appropriate and effective moment to speak aloud. Groups can experiment with repetitions, echoes and pauses making their own improvised effects.

We can add meaning and depth to still images or freeze-frames by writing characters' thoughts on pieces of paper and placing them in the images as in comic strips and photo-stories. Appropriately shaped laminated thought-bubbles are a very cheap and useful resources as they can be wiped clean and used time and time again.

Thought-tracking: passing thoughts

In this variant of thought-tracking a character stands in the centre of a circle. Individual members of the class take it in turns to cross the circle speaking aloud the thoughts of the character as they pass.

Making meaning through sound

Choral speaking

Choral Speaking involves a group of people speaking together for dramatic effect. They may speak in unison or experiment with a mixture of single and multiple voices. The key elements of choral speaking are volume, tempo, tone, vocal register, pause and rhythm.

Soundscape/sound collage

Working in small groups people are asked to make a pattern of sound which might illustrate something or someone in a drama. This is a way of making meaning which could 'allow' language as well as sounds but is more likely to rely on sound effects. Groups need to experiment with ways of making non-verbal sounds, for example, using:

→ their mouths (sighing, whistling, breathing, cheering);

→ other parts of their bodies (stamping feet, clapping hands);

→ 'found' sounds (a piece of paper slowly ripped or screwed up, a pen rattling on a radiator, a door squeak);

→ percussion (improvised or conventional musical instruments).

Soundscapes/sound collages are often performed to audiences who have their eyes shut to ensure only an aural focus.

Voice collage

The voice collage is a variant of the soundscape in which only vocal effects are allowed. This approach is more likely to 'allow' language to be included alongside other vocal effects.

Making meaning through movement

Mime

In mime we are using our bodies to interact with imaginary objects, people, locations and audiences. Working in mime has a number of practical advantages. First it can be immediate and by definition requires no props or setting. Second mime can focus us on visual and kinaesthetic communication (stripping away verbal communication) as it relies on only gesture, facial expression and movement. Third it is something that all children naturally do in their play and even older students often experience a sense of pleasure in being allowed to 'equip' their work from the store rooms of their own imaginations.

Expressive movement/dance drama

Movement work in drama can easily cross a line into dance. By adding music or percussion to activities such as essence machines, transitions, storyboards movement work can become more theatrical and expressive. Classes who are used to expressing themselves in more formal movement styles will often ask for music to accompany their work. Sometimes the work is set up as dance drama and the boundaries are intentionally merged (Figure 3.4).

Figure 3.4 Expressive movement. Photograph courtesy of Steven Beaumont
(professional photographer, www.stevenbeaumont.com)

'Move if . . .'

This simple strategy can be used at the start of a drama to make links between past, real experiences and the themes and issues in the drama that is about to unfold. It invites engagement and encourages empathy. The participants stand in a circle and the teacher makes a series of statements starting with. 'Move if . . .'. All those to whom the statement applies must move to a different point in the circle. For example (Unit 5), a drama about migration opens with a number of 'move if' statements which require the participants to think about their real life experiences of travel, leaving home and separation. This is an active, personal but safe way of opening the door to engagement with the drama.

Working in role

Drawing/designing/writing/mapping/enquiring/researching in Role

In these activities people carry out tasks 'as if' they were someone else. When working in this way they are required to imagine and respond authentically to situations and tasks, from within the role (Figure 3.5).

Mantle of the Expert

In this strategy (which some now consider to be a curriculum 'approach') participants in the drama are 'given' roles which carry assumed expertise and responsibilities. Although even young children will know that this expertise is imagined and not real the tasks set from within the mantle (often commissioned by an external client) can empower, raise self-esteem and performance, improve motivation and elevate both focus and seriousness of purpose. Mantle of the Expert (MoE) roles in these drama units include trusted advisors to the King, expert

Figure 3.5 Drawing in role

rat-catchers, officials from the Ministry of Food, advertising copywriters and top poster designers.

Telling stories

Active story-telling

This form of physical theatre requires the class either individually or in groups to respond to a narrative by 'becoming' objects and characters as they crop up in the story. The whole group becomes a constantly changing physical shape which can represent geographical features, animals, objects and of course people.

Eavesdropping (see 'tracking thoughts')

This strategy can be used to allow a large number of people to contribute fragments of narrative detail to a collective drama. For example, if people working in pairs have been improvising in role, the teacher can ask the class to all be still and silent until the teacher seamlessly passes by each pair in turn. When the teacher passes by each pair, it will be their opportunity to go back and re-enact what they have already enacted or they might carry on improvising from where they left off. When the teacher passes on the pair falls silent and still again and it will be another pairs' turn. The teacher may only stay 'eavesdropping' for a minute or so. This can also be done with small groups.

Teacher narration: first person

Here the teacher takes on the role of a character in the drama and narrates using a first person narrative. *'I sat down on my throne and looked around at my ministers'*.

Teacher narration: third person

Here a teacher introduces or advances the narrative acting as a storyteller and using a third person authorial voice. *'The King sat down on his throne and looked around at his Ministers.'* Often a teacher will try to incorporate ideas supplied by class members into the narration, so that the children hear their ideas as part of a successful narrative.

Improvising

Improvisation involves expression (verbal or non-verbal) which is spontaneous and un-rehearsed. Much of the time when we interact with others in role in drama we are required to improvise and it is the immediacy of this expression which can make drama feel 'real' and exciting. Genuinely spontaneous improvisation can be very effectively shared with audiences however there is also a place for using improvisation as a basis for devising and scripting rehearsed work to be performed for others.

Devising and performing

The showing of work (or the preparation of work to be shown) in drama introduces a different dynamic, makes different demands and promotes different learning. In improvisation we were in the first instance making meaning for ourselves as participants. The introduction of a performance element means that we must now make meaning for others. Often when the time comes to present an improvisation to the whole class a group will want to refine and improve the 'script' or change the shape of the original improvisation so that an audience will have a better view. In thinking about how an audience is likely to perceive, understand and evaluate their work, groups will start to make artistic decisions which are essentially communicative. In devising work for performance a working checklist could include questions such as:

→ Will they understand what we mean?

→ Will they know who we are?

→ Will they be able to see everything we're showing them and hear what we're saying?

→ Can we find a better, stronger/sadder/funnier/more powerful way to communicate our ideas?

Forum theatre

In 'forum theatre' the 'play' can be negotiated and purposefully changed through a dialogue between actors and audiences. The audience are encouraged to join the actors in helping them to solve their character's problems and resolve their difficulties by trying different behaviours, speech and actions.

Forum theatre can be used in a drama to:

→ work towards the resolution of a problem or issue;

→ hear, see and examine both sides of an argument;

→ consider alternative courses of action and their impact on self and others;

→ consider the impact of the different uses of language;

→ examine motivation, why people say and do certain things and what impact this can have on others and on situations;

→ discuss why some people have power and others don't and whether and how this can be positively changed;

→ help characters to behave and feel differently and experience the possible changes this can make to themselves and the situations they are in (linking cause and effect).

In making 'forum theatre' we need:

A forum	A defined space/place where the discussions and investigations will take place. This could be a stage or simply be a space in the middle of the room.
A 'play'	This might be improvised or scripted dialogue, a moment in a drama, a movement sequence or even a still image. Normally the passage under investigation will be quite short and will have been prepared for presentation and scrutiny.
Actors	To show the 'play'.
An audience	To observe the play and respond to it.
'Spect-actors'	Who join in the play sometimes only partially by suggesting ideas from their seats in the audience or sometimes by getting up and joining the actors in the performance space to work with or as them.
A facilitator (sometimes called 'the joker')	Who 'manages', facilitates and mediates the interventions and discussions. This critical role is usually undertaken by a teacher.
Rules	The facilitator needs to set out clear rules for intervention.

Many types of audience intervention can happen in 'forum theatre'; some of the key ways in which a member of the audience can contribute to the forum and become a 'spect-actor' are through:

INVESTIGATING/CHALLENGING	Questioning characters who then answer in role.
RESTAGING	Suggesting alternative actions for the characters to try that may lead to a different response and outcome.
REWRITING	Suggesting different things the characters could say that may lead to a change of outcome when other characters respond.
REINFORCING	Coming into the performance space and helping a character to make a point or win an argument by working alongside them in the role.
REPLACING	Taking the place of a character (substitution) and showing how that character could behave differently.

PART 2
DRAMA UNITS

Introduction

The Units

The units in this section have been designed to:

→ Develop engaging fictions which can be entered by the whole class in role.

→ Present participants with problems to be solved, decisions to be made and issues to be resolved from inside the drama.

→ Offer the opportunity for participants in role to influence the course of a drama's narrative development and eventual resolution.

→ Provide context and pretext for over a hundred writing opportunities.

Using the unit grids

Although the drama units in this section provide clearly signposted routes through the eight dramas, teachers should feel free to adapt, adjust, omit and insert in order to make both the resources and the units themselves appropriate to their own teaching contexts and the needs of their classes. Teachers may choose to follow a step-by-step route through a drama or use the grids to design their own routes, focussing on particular strategies and writing opportunities. Each grid can be developed into an extended scheme of work lasting several weeks or can be used to provide teaching and learning opportunities for a single lesson. Some activities could even be used in isolation as part of an English lesson although engagement and the motivation to write is likely to be higher when the drama is sustained.

Reading, speaking, listening and writing

Drama offers a uniquely active way to integrate reading, writing, speaking and listening. Each of the drama units enables pupils to read, speak, listen and write as 'in role' participants in 'live' fictions and to draw on things they have read, spoken and heard when they come to write in and/or out of role. The drama also provides an emotionally engaging and 'real' purpose for the writing.

Challenge and support

Many of the drama activities and writing opportunities are signposted with **C** or **S** symbols which respectively designate **C**hallenge or **S**upport.

Challenge activities which may require more thought or a greater level of skill have been designed to make more complex demands on pupils. A decision to use a challenge activity might be based on the age of the pupils or on their experience and confidence as drama participants.

Support activities are not necessarily easier but will often include 'scaffolding' activities which will provide a clearer and more secure route towards an objective.

The writing opportunities

The drama units in this section develop situations, narratives and imagined experiences which clearly establish pretexts and contexts for writing. These writing tasks provide opportunities to:

→ write from the perspective of an imagined role;

→ write purposefully with a specific reader or audience in mind;

→ practice writing for a wide range of purposes;

→ practice different types of writing in a wide range of genres and formats;

→ develop written texts working alone or in groups.

There are also opportunities for adults to work in role as co-writers, sharing and guiding the writing.

Creating your own resources

Finally, the authors of this book encourage teachers to consider creating their own drama and writing resources. To all teachers who have experienced the time-consuming and frustrating task of searching in vain for the perfect poem, article or extract from a novel to inspire, support or illustrate a particular lesson we would say, 'Why not do it yourself and write your own?'

Key

C = Drama strategies and writing tasks which are more **Challenging**.

S = Drama strategies and writing tasks where more **Support** is provided.

UNIT 1
Mary Maguire: Housemaid

Introduction

In this unit – set in late Victorian England – we step inside the troubled world of 17-year-old housemaid Mary Maguire. Although lucky to have a secure job in a prestigious house Mary is restless, unfulfilled and exhausted by the relentless drudgery of the work. When an opportunity to escape and start a new life presents itself Mary has some difficult decisions to make.

Themes

→ Duty

→ Work

→ Freedom

→ Family

→ Conformity

→ Love

→ Status and power

Writing opportunities

→ Collective writing

→ Text edit and composition

→ Lists

→ Interior monologues

→ Titles and captions

→ Script writing

→ Audience Response Reports

→ Descriptive writing

→ Personification

→ Character study

→ Persuasive writing

→ Discursive writing

→ Alternative endings

Writing Resources (pp. 152–9)

→ WR1: Housemaids 1890

→ WR2: Mary Maguire poem

→ WR3: Domestic service 1897 – some facts

→ WR4: Rules for domestic staff

→ WR5: Mary Maguire's reference

→ WR6: Advertisement for a housemaid

→ WR7: Fragments from Mary's diary

→ WR8: A letter from Arthur (hidden in a box)

Other resources

Essential: sentence strips, adhesive labels
Optional: drum

Mary Maguire: Housemaid

Activity	Drama strategy	Purpose	Teacher guidance	Writing opportunities
1.	Teacher narration	→ To introduce – theme – central character – tension → To focus attention on key words	Read the poem, Mary Maguire **(WR2: p. 153)** to the class. Invite the class to listen to the poem with their eyes closed. Read it slowly. *Imagine what it would be like to be Mary.* Allow some silent reflection time.	
2.	Statement prompts ('I wonder')	→ To encourage curiosity → To offer shared ownership → To open up a range of possible narratives	Invite the class to share what they would like to know more about by speaking sentences which start with the words *'I wonder . . .'*. **S.** We might model this by providing an *'I wonder . . .'* of our own, for example *'I wonder if the mistress has noticed that Mary is so happy that day'.*	**Collective writing** The 'I wonder . . .' sentences can be collated on a whiteboard or on adhesive labels and then arranged a a collective list which could be read as a poem.
3.	Choral reading	→ To encourage focus on the poem at word level → To 'enter' the poem actively (individually and collectively) → To experiment with making meaning using chosen fragments	Each pupil is given a copy of the poem **(WR2, p. 153)** and asked to *'underline 8 words which you think are important'*. Read the poem very slowly again inviting people to join in as each of their underlined words crop up.	**Text edit and composition** Peop now transfer their eight chosen words onto slips of paper and organize them into new 'poems' of their own. Experimenting with shape, structure and sequence they arrange their own eight-word versions on the floor. Individual clas members can then explore the roo to examine, interpret and discuss these versions.
4.	Teacher in Role (TiR)/collective role	→ To step into the drama from a specific character's perspective → To develop tension → To advance a shared narrative → To illustrate the stark social hierarchy of the time	Before starting the scene it might be useful to examine and discuss **WR1, 2, 3 and 4 (pp. 152–5).** When looking at these resources ask the class to *make a note of things you find surprising or interesting or anything that makes you feel annoyed or sad.* The **TiR** is the mistress of the house. As mistress we must make it clear that it is Mrs Braithwaite's responsibility to select and train staff and so it is her job to sort out this problem.	**List of prompts to support improvisation** **S.** The key points that Mrs Braithwaite must put across to Mary could be listed and displayed as prompts before moving on to Activity 5.

Activity	Drama strategy	Purpose	Teacher guidance	Writing opportunities
			Mrs Braithwaite must be very clear. Mary must understand that if her attitude doesn't improve she will lose her job. The collective role of the class is Mrs Braithwaite, the Housekeeper. This might be a good time to study some of the rules for domestic staff **(WR4, p. 155)**. The **TiR** here is a high status character and needs to make it clear that she (the mistress) is very angry and disappointed. The mistress has noticed that Mary Maguire (an excellent servant until now) has started behaving insolently. Mary has been seen smiling to herself and smirking and has even been heard humming when guests were present. The class together in role as Mrs Braithwaite are asked to speak to Mary Maguire immediately and warn her about her behaviour.

S. If your class has not used collective role before you may need to practice this strategy before embarking on the scene. See the **Drama Strategies** for more detailed guidelines. | |
| 5. | **Collective role**

TiR

Voice soundtrack | → To 'meet' the central character
→ To provide opportunity for class members to use and consolidate material emerging in the drama. There may also be an opportunity to advance narrative and build tension | Continuing in their collective role as Mrs Braithwaite the class must now address the teacher in role as Mary. Now their collective role (Mrs Braithwaite) has high status and the **TiR** (Mary) has low status. Before starting this scene it might be helpful to read aloud the extract from Mary's diary dated Sunday 11th December **(WR7, p. 158)**. The **TiR** (Mary) needs to deny that anything is 'going on' and although she claims to be unaware that she has been insolent it might be useful to see a slight streak of insolence in her demeanour.

C. Interior monologues (voice soundtrack)

Having written the interior monologues, the scene between Mary and Mrs Braithwaite can now be replayed with one of the small groups reading aloud their interior monologues as an accompanying soundtrack. | **Interior monologue**

The class are asked to write down the thoughts which might have been going through Mary's head during this meeting with Mrs Braithwaite. Then in smaller groups (fours) they are asked to bring together these thoughts into a single piece of writing (Mary's interior monologue). |

Activity	Drama strategy	Purpose	Teacher guidance	Writing opportunities
6.	**Teacher narration** **Still image** **(whole class)**	→ To create a symbolic physical representation of a character's emotions → To encourage empathy	You might read or improvise a very brief passage of **teacher narration** such as '. . .*There were a million things that Mary wanted to say to Mrs Braithwaite. She wanted to scream at them at the top of her voice and storm out of the room and slam the door. But she didn't. She couldn't. Mary politely curtsied to Mrs Braithwaite, walked slowly out of the room and quietly shut the door behind her.*' Working as a whole class we now build one still collective image of Mary at this moment. Joining the shape one by one each person freezes in a position which portrays Mary's feelings.	**Captions writing** A digital photograph of this shape could be taken. Titles and captions can be added.
7.	**Thought-tracking**	→ To give voice to a character's thoughts and feelings in preparation for shared writing	The still image is recreated but this time as each person enters the shape she speaks aloud a word or phrase which sums up Mary's thoughts or feelings at this moment.	**Collective (shared) writing and poetry** Each class member writes the thought which she brought to the image on a blank sentence strip. In groups of six they organize these strips into a poem. **Individual writing** **C.** Using the 'thought strip poem' (above) as a writing frame, the poem can be extended further by individual pupils and the range of resulting poems shared or performed afterwards.
8.	**Role on the wall**	→ To audit what we know about the central character → To set an agenda for further exploration of the character	Class members are asked three questions: 1. What do we *know* about Mary? 2. What do we *think we know* about Mary? 3. What do we *need to find out about Mary*? We (or they) can scribe these on the board. Alternatively we can define three spaces in the room (one corresponding to each question) and invite the class to each enter one of three defined spaces and offer a statement aloud. **S.** We may need to provide a model of each of these statements e.g. *1. 'I know Mary is smiling sometimes.' 2. 'I think I know she is a bit defiant.' 3. 'I want to know if she'll get the sack.'*	**Role on the wall** An outline of Mary can be drawn and the pupils can write what they know, think they know or want to know about her in areas around the outline. If this is done on self-adhesive, removable labels they can be moved or removed at other points in the drama once we learn more about her.

Activity	Drama strategy	Purpose	Teacher guidance	Writing opportunities
			C. We can challenge some of the statements made by asking people to justify why they think they know something or to explain why they want to find something out.	
9.	**Image theatre**	→ To reflect on the differences and contradictions between Mary's public and private lives → To bring to life, the job expectations placed on Mary	In groups of three the class is asked to create two collective images. **Image 1**. Mary as Mrs Braithwaite would like her to *behave (the ideal)*. **Image 2**. Mary as she is really feeling *(the reality)*. Then the groups are asked to move in slow motion from shape 1 to shape 2. A drum beat can be used to provide rhythmic structure for these movement pieces. Groups can be given a certain number of beats within which they must complete the transition. **C.** The 'ideal' and the 'reality' could be depicted as short scenes the pupils create in pairs or small groups.	**Scriptwriting (dialogue)** An imagined scene between the two Mary's. Mary A (*ideal*) tries to persuade Mary B (*reality*) to behave appropriately to keep her job. Mary B will emphatically resist this. These short scripts can be created by individuals, pairs or small groups and passed to others to perform. The scriptwriters can elect to direct their scripted scenes or let others direct them.
10.	**Performance carousel**	→ To enable group members to watch and reflect on a range of responses to the same task	The carousel starts with the groups standing in neutral (standing still arms at sides) in a large circle. You will decide which group will start and in which direction the carousel will turn (clockwise or anti-clockwise). You can cue the opening with the first beat of your drum. As each group completes its slow motion transition and freezes the next group will start. Each group can be paired with another group and asked to remember what they have seen. They are told before watching that they may need to share three things they liked about the scene/shapes and one thing that they wish to be improved.	**Audience Response Reports** Working individually the class is asked to write about the performance of the group with which they were paired. **S.** The writing can be supported by the following prompts: → write three things we liked about it; → identify one thing that might improve it. **C.** Additionally pupils can be asked to describe in writing the transition they have seen.
11.	**Soundscape**	→ To gain a more vivid sense of Mary's daily experience → To highlight an auditory perspective which can then support descriptive writing	In groups of six the class are asked to make a **soundscape** of Mary's working life. They can use mouth sounds (whistling, groaning, singing, sighing, etc., but no language is allowed) and any objects they can find in the room to make noises that illustrate Mary's day. Groups will perform their sound collages to the rest of the class who will listen with their eyes closed.	**Descriptive writing** Students start by listing some of the noises they have made and heard. They then turn this list into either a poem or a piece of descriptive prose. **S.** We might model this by offering a couple of first lines: 'a clock ticks in the hallway'; 'boots stamp heavily up a wooden staircase'. The writing can be done collectively in groups or as an individual exercise.

Activity	Drama strategy	Purpose	Teacher guidance	Writing opportunities
			Groups should be encouraged to experiment with the proxemics of the sound (i.e. how the meaning of sounds can be altered by their placement, direction and movement).	
			S. A way to model this before they embark on this task is to ask the class to sit on the floor in a space, shut their eyes and listen. Move quickly around the space letting them listen to our footsteps approaching and moving away. Make random sounds close to and further removed from people.	
			Two important safety net rules should be agreed here. In performances when audience have eyes closed no one should be touched and no loud noises should be made close to anyone's ears.	
12.	Talking objects	→ To deepen understanding of personification → To learn more about a character → To build narrative	Ask the class to sit around the edges of the space. Explain that you are going to find out more about Mary and her life by meeting and talking to some of the objects in her room. The space in the middle will now become Mary's attic bedroom. Explain that some objects such as furniture are static and will only ever see what's in front of them. Others such as shoes, hats may get out more!	**Personification** **C.** A short piece of prose (or verse) can be written from the object's perspective following Activity 12. If these are put together as a series, a collective writing piece can emerge which exemplifies personification.
			S. A good way to model this strategy is to explain that you are going to be the door. It's not necessary to try to represent the object's shape but to just place ourself where that object would be and answer questions in role, from the object's perspective. Ask the class to think what they might be able to learn from Mary by questioning a door. Answer their questions very seriously. Then invite class members to enter into the room (through the door!) place themselves in the space and say what object they are. About six to eight objects is enough.	
			The class can then hot-seat (ask questions of) the objects, who will answer in role.	

Activity	Drama strategy	Purpose	Teacher guidance	Writing opportunities
13.	Reading in role	→ To review some of the text extracts in order to develop a more complex and interesting narrative	**C.** Split class into groups of six and give out copies of **WR5** (Mary's reference), **WR7** (Fragments from Mary's diary) and **WR8** (Arthur's letter). Ask the groups to discuss how it might sound if the person who wrote these words read them aloud. We need to think about the status, social class and confidence of each of the writers. Give time for the groups to experiment and practice before listening to different readings and interpretations of the extracts. **S.** If you don't have readers who are confident enough to read aloud in this way you may have to read the extracts yourself. A discussion might now consider what sort of man Arthur seems to be (based on the texts) and could make a list of questions they would ask him if they had a chance to meet him. Do they trust this man? Why/why not? What do they need to find out before deciding if they trust him? **S.** Ask the class to make lists of questions for Arthur. What do we need to find out? What are the best questions to ask?	**Writing for a specific audience** Using **WRs 5, 7** and **8** on **pages 156**, **158** and **159** as models, the brief here is to write a new piece of text which could fit into this drama. Options include: → a new entry in Mary's diary → another letter from Arthur. **C.** An updated employer reference for Mary written by Mrs Braithwaite.
14.	TiR	→ To find out more about a key character	Explain that the class will now have an opportunity to meet and question Arthur. The **TiR** here needs to offer some real balance so that Mary's decision about leaving is as difficult as possible. If Arthur is clearly an uncaring cad then we make her decision an easy one. If however he's a sensitive devoted soul who loves her and will obviously make her happy then again we make her decision too easy. Probably the best way to play it is to make him a nice guy who just hasn't thought through the consequences of what he's suggesting. His view should be that *'everything will be alright . . . we'll find a way to help out Mary's family . . . it doesn't matter if Mary leaves and has no references . . . haven't really thought about weddings yet but it will probably be quite soon . . .'*	**Character appraisal** **C.** On the basis of this meeting ask the class to write a brief character appraisal. What do we know about this man? How do we feel about him? On what do we base our judgements? **S.** The writing can be supported by a writing frame for example. Name/Age/Physical Appearance/Good Points (Strengths)/Bad Points (Weaknesses)/Things he Said/Conclusion. Should Mary trust this man? **Role on the wall** The information and opinions about Arthur could be gathered simply on self-adhesive labels around an outline of Arthur.
	Reading in role			

Activity	Drama strategy	Purpose	Teacher guidance	Writing opportunities
			Ideally our class will divide over this role. Some may be supportive of Arthur in his attempt to woo Mary away from the Big House. Others may see him as a threat to her.	
15.	Writing in role	→ To construct an argument in favour of a particular course of action	Mary is trying to make up her mind whether or not to walk away from her job in the Big House. Class members are asked to imagine that they are someone in whom Mary has secretly confided; a friend perhaps or relative or fellow servant.	**Persuasive writing** The brief is to write a letter to Mary telling her what we think she should do and why.
	Improvisation	→ To write from the perspective of a character in order to give the writing purpose and direction		**S.** A shorter and less demanding activity could involve writing a short note or message to Mary as her confidante (rather than a full letter).
	Eavesdropping		**S.** Prior to the writing activity there could be an improvisation task. Working in pairs as Mary and her friend pupils improvise a conversation in which Mary asks for advice about what she should do. Later we can enable the whole class to listen to these conversations by walking round the space activating each of the conversations by stopping beside them.	
16.	Reading in role	→ To share key elements of the letters (or notes)	Pupils are asked to choose one or two lines from the letter or note they've just written. They should be the best lines, the lines they think are most important, the ones which are most likely to persuade Mary towards a particular course of action. Then go around the class and hear aloud the selected lines, spoken persuasively.	
17.	Conscience alley	→ To set out and evaluate opposing arguments in a formal ritual	The class is asked to divide into two groups. Those who argued that Mary should stay on one side of the room and those who argued she should go on the other. The two groups form lines facing each other. In the first instance you walk slowly between the lines and as you pass by each person speaks to you the lines that have been selected from the letters and notes in 16. When you get to the end of the line announce which argument you feel is stronger and most persuasive. **Stress though that this is only your view.** Put the arguments to the test again by inviting individuals to experience and respond to the walk through the alley.	**Discursive writing** **C.** A conscience alley enables the pros and cons of a course of action to come into the open and be heard aloud by all. This can provide a helpful model for discursive writing. The brief here is to discuss Mary's situation considering both sides of the '(leave/stay)' argument arriving finally at a firm conclusion.

ctivity	Drama strategy	Purpose	Teacher guidance	Writing opportunities
8.	Storyboards	→ To enable groups to create and present a range of alternative endings or next stages in the narrative	In his letter Arthur says that he will wait for Mary by the gates on Sunday. It's now Sunday afternoon. Groups of four are asked to make a storyboard sequence (with no more than four still images) which shows clearly what Mary has decided to do. Does Mary join Arthur? And if so is she carrying her case? Show us what happens through a sequence of up to four images. **C.** We could ask that the four images are each just a few seconds apart in time or else years apart in time. The storyboards can be shared in turn and interpreted by the audience.	**Alternative endings for the story** The brief here is to write a single paragraph which finishes this story. **S.** We might want to offer a starting sentence, e.g. *'It was Sunday afternoon and the clock in the hall struck two . . .'* **Alternative texts** **C.** Once an ending has been decided upon it can be communicated to a reader through a number of writing formats including: → a description of a scene → a piece of dialogue → an employer's reference written later by the mistress → a later entry in Mary's diary → a letter from Mary to Arthur (or vice versa) → an additional verse to be added to the Mary Maguire poem **(WR2, p. 153)**.

UNIT 2
The King's Daughters

Introduction

This unit – which examines some of the characters and themes of Shakespeare's play King Lear – can be used as an off-text introduction to the play. However the unit also stands as an independent drama in its own right exploring the dark world of an unpredictable elderly king, his deeply troubled daughters and a state which is just about to fall apart.

Themes

→ Power and authority

→ Jealousy

→ Ageing

→ Parenting

→ Sibling rivalry

→ Honesty

→ Love

Writing opportunities

→ Text edit

→ Collaborative poetry

→ Thought collage

→ Print journalism: front page leader

→ Persuasive writing

→ Street graffiti

→ Recording thoughts/feelings

→ Collaborative writing in role

→ Eye witness statements

→ Print journalism: Vox Pop

→ Diary writing

→ Letter writing

Writing Resources (pp. 160–5)

→ WR1: Termly school reports: Goneril, Regan and Cordelia

→ WR2: Message to the King's advisers

→ WR3a and b: Headlines from *The Daily Realm*

→ WR4: Diary extracts, January 13th: Goneril, Regan and Cordelia

→ WR5: The three speeches: word boxes

→ WR6: Extract from Shakespeare's King Lear

Other resources

Essential: Sheets of flip chart paper. Marker pens (different colours)
Optional: Drum

The King's Daughters

Activity	Drama strategy	Purpose	Teacher guidance	Opportunities for writing
1.	Introduction	→ To establish the setting for the drama	We will need to explain that this is the story of a king and his three daughters and that we are going to explore the beginning of this story and find out for ourselves what happens and maybe write our own ending. Depending on the learning objectives set for this unit we might want to explain that Shakespeare used the same idea for the opening of one of his most famous plays and that it might be interesting at some point to have a look at Shakespeare's play and see if his story turned out like-ours.	
2.	Reading in role	→ To introduce three of the four central characters	Explain that the first thing we are going to look at is a document that was written a long time before our story starts. The three girls we are going to look at are princesses. They are the daughters of a very powerful king. Their school reports **(WR1, p. 160)** were written when Goneril, Regan and Cordelia were respectively 12,10 and 8. **S.** You may decide to read the reports yourself as a Teacher in Role **(TiR)** . . . **C.** . . . or alternatively invite members of the class to read.	**Text edit** Split class into groups of three giving each group a copy of the three reports. Groups must choose ten words from each of the three reports which sum up the child being described. They must write their ten words on a sheet of paper in three columns ; one for each of the daughters. We can display these word lists for sharing, comparison and discussion.
3.	Role sculpture (whole group)	→ To create a physical representation of each of the three children	Working as a whole class announce which role is to be shaped and ask people to come into a central space one by one. Once into the space each person must make a still shape which depicts something about the character which they have learnt from the school report. **S.** We can support this task by suggesting that people concentrate on one of the words chosen in their text edit or . . .	**Collaborative poetry writing** In the same groups write three short poems. Each poem must give a vivid picture of the child it describes. Poems should be no longer than 20 words. **S.** Ten of those words should be those chosen in the previous exercise. **C.** None of the chosen words can be used.

Activity	Drama strategy	Purpose	Teacher guidance	Opportunities for writing
			C. . . . ask them to think of a specific phrase from the report. Repeat the process for each of the reports so that we have three role sculptures. We can return to these at any time to 're-capture' the three roles although we may want to adapt the sculptures as we learn more about the characters.	
4.	**'Casting'**	→ To hand responsibility for the development of one of the characters to the participants → To develop team work	From now on group members will be part of one of three collective roles. These collectives are teams which are responsible for the character's actions, speech and decisions. Casting membership of the collective roles needs planning and almost certainly teacher direction. Ideally we would want three equally sized groups of equal ability. This might be a good reason for us to cast the collective roles ourself.	
5.	**Role sculpture (character groups)**	→ To give members of the collective role to work together as a 'specialist' team → To develop a shared understanding and ownership of the character	Ask the class to sit in their three groups and talk about the role which they are going to develop together. **S.** '*Tell each other how you feel about this character. What do you admire about her? What do you dislike? How would you feel about her if she was in your class? Remember that you don't have to like a character in order to pretend to be her.*' Give each of the three groups a space to work in. Each member of the collective role will now enter their space in turn. As they freeze into a still shape depicting their role they must say a single word or phrase which they believe sums up the character. They may choose to re-use the word or phrase they were thinking of in strategy 3 or use something which emerged from the discussion.	
6.	**Human keyboard**	→ To highlight key words and make them memorable through performance	We can activate the chosen words and phrases by tapping group members on their shoulders. When tapped each person will speak their chosen words. Shoulders become keys on a keyboard. Interesting effects can be achieved by repeating the same 'note' or playing two notes at the same time. Invite members of other collectives to play the keyboard. Experiment with two players (four hands) or three players (six hands).	**Thought collage. Interior monologue** Members of the collective are asked to write their chosen words/phrases onto cards. They are then tasked as a group with forming them into a collage on the floor. They are asked to think about the ways in which space and shape might add meaning to the words which they set out.

ctivity	Drama strategy	Purpose	Teacher guidance	Opportunities for writing
			C. Invite the 'keyboards' to play themselves. In this variation no hands activate the 'keys'. Groups can experiment with repetitions, echoes and pauses making their own improvised effects.	Then as individuals they are asked to imagine that their character is sitting in a school classroom and daydreaming. The writing task is to write the thoughts that are going through the character's head. S. We could provide a prompt such as *'I wish I was somewhere else right now. I wish . . .'*
.	**Teacher narration** **Mantle of the Expert (MoE)**	→ To advance the story into the 'present' and to introduce dramatic tension	Ask the class to stand in a space alone and to shut their eyes. As soon as all eyes are shut start placing copies of **WR2 (p. 161)** on the floor in front of each of them. Use the following words to develop the narrative (or better still make up your own version). *'Those school reports were written a long time and the three girls have now grown up. Goneril is now 22, Regan 20 and Cordelia 18. Their father is called King Lear. He is now an old man. He rules the country helped by a group of very wise and trusted advisers called the Inner Chamber. One night each member of the Inner Chamber receives a message. The message is slipped under their front door late at night. 'You are a member of that Inner Chamber;' a very wise person who for many years has given the King good advice. Open your eyes. Your message has arrived. Pick it up and read.* As they are reading it might be useful for the class to hear your voice reading it too.	
.	**a. Thought-tracking** **b. Rumours and eavesdropping**	→ To help group members engage with their new role and the responsibilities which it carries	Ask the class to think about their first reactions on reading the message. Tell the class that you are going to walk around the space and stop in front of individual members of the Inner Chamber who will then speak their thoughts. **S.** We can provide more support for the class by using an 'I wonder' strategy (see **Drama Strategies**).	**Print journalism. Writing to inform in role** Explain that news of the secret meeting has leaked out and the newspapers are very intrigued. The class are journalists writing for a national daily, *The Daily Realm*. Their brief now is to complete the piece by telling their readers about some of the rumours which are flying about.

Activity	Drama strategy	Purpose	Teacher guidance	Opportunities for writing
			Ask members of the Inner Chamber to work in pairs. Although they have been ordered not to talk to anyone about the meeting they secretly talk to a fellow member about why the King might have called this meeting. After a while call for silence. Walk around the space stopping in front of pairs. This will be a cue for that pair to restart their conversation as you (and the rest of the class) eavesdrop. **S.** Here are some statement prompts which might help pairs to get their conversations going. *'I think the King wants to see us because. . .' or* *'I've heard that the King wants to see us because . . .'*	**S.** Give our journalists copies of **WR3A (p. 161)** telling them that they have already written their headline and the first paragraph of tomorrow's front page story. The journalists now have a writing frame to work from. **C.** Set the same writing task without access to **WR3A (p. 161)**
9.	**Statement prompts** **('I remember . . .')** **TiR/MoE**	→ To advance the narrative, introduce a problem to be solved and develop tension	Remind the class members of their responsibilities as members of the Inner Chamber. Their job is to always watch very carefully and tell the King if they think he is about to do something wrong. In the past the Inner Chamber has stopped the King from making some very dangerous mistakes. The history of the King's previous errors of judgement can be sketched in using an **'I remember . . .'** strategy. Members of the Inner Chamber sit in a circle. One by one they recall incidents standing up and starting with the words *'I remember the time when the King . . .'* **TiR** as King Lear talks to class as members of the Inner Chamber **(MoE).** In this **TiR** the King will inform the Inner Chamber that he intends to resign (abdicate) from his throne and divide the kingdom into three giving each of his daughters a third share. He plans to do this tomorrow at a special ceremony at which each of his daughters must make a speech about their love for their father.	**Diary writing** The task here is to write a diary in role as a Member for the Inner Chamber in which the Member describes how he felt when the King made his announcement at the meeting.

Activity	Drama strategy	Purpose	Teacher guidance	Opportunities for writing
			The size of their share of the kingdom will depend on how much they say they love him. The **TiR** here is a provocative role aimed to encourage the group members to challenge the plan which is revealed. The King **TiR** must be very pleased with his plan and adopt a 'what can go wrong' approach. **S.** If group members can see no flaw in the plans you may need to suggest that the Inner Chamber hold a private meeting to discuss the 'magnificent plan'. We can attend this meeting in a separate **TiR** as a sceptical Inner Chamber Member. Hopefully however class members will see that dividing up the kingdom with three armies and three rulers is a flawed idea particularly if we have already established that this King has a tendency to make foolish mistakes. .	
10.	Image theatre Performance carousel	→ To clarify the arguments against dividing up the kingdom	Groups of four or five are asked to create three still images showing the things that could go wrong if the state is divided up. You could use a drum beat to move in slow motion transition between the three images. These transition sequences can be shared with the whole group through a **performance carousel.**	**Persuasive writing in role** **C.** Here in role as members of the Inner Chamber the task is to write a letter to the King trying to persuade him to change his mind about dividing up the kingdom. The letters might draw his attention to some of the fears depicted in the images we have just observed.
11.	Teacher narration Reading in role	→ To examine (out of role) the responses of the three daughters to their father's decision	Narrate '*the King has called the three daughters to his rooms and informed them of his decision to divide up the kingdom. We don't know exactly what was said at that meeting but we do have a fragment of the diary written later that night by each of the daughters.*' Ask the class to go back to their three collective Goneril/Regan/Cordelia groups and give each collective a copy of its own diary extract **(WR4, p. 162)**. Ask someone in each group to read the entry in role and give the whole class a minute's silent thinking time.	

Activity	Drama strategy	Purpose	Teacher guidance	Opportunities for writing
12.	**TiR/three collective roles** (see *Drama Strategies*)	→ To engage with the King's decision in role and to experience differing responses to that decision	Explain to the class that we are now going to go back a few hours in time and witness that meeting which is described in the diary fragments. The three daughters have been summoned to meet the King. They don't know why. The King has something important to tell them. Ask members of the collective roles to sit closely together. Remind them of that when we do a collective role we to speak as 'I' not 'we' and imagine that a single person not a group which is speaking to the King. The **TiR** as King Lear needs to start by explaining his decision to divide up the kingdom giving each of his daughters a share the size of which will depend on how much they say they love him. He needs to apologize to Goneril who as eldest might have imagined that she would inherit the whole kingdom but tell her that this way is better and that we're sure she'll understand. Now the **TiR** needs to ask each of the collective roles for their opinions and responses. The **TiR** may listen to any objections but he will not change his mind.	**Street graffiti (writing in role)** Word has somehow got out that the King is planning to divide the kingdom into three. Many people in the country are bitterly opposed to this. Overnight walls in the city are scrawled with 'one nation' slogans. Fix large sheets of paper to the walls of the room to set up a graffiti wall and invite group members to take on roles as One Nation activists who come out at night and write and draw on the city walls. Remind them that this activity is illegal and if caught they will be arrested. They will need to be quick and they can't afford to waste words. Allow a 3-minute thinking/planning time and supply different colour marker pens.
13.	**Role on the wall**	→ To examine the feelings of the three princesses at this point in the drama and to find language record those feelings	The outline or image of each of the three princesses is put on the wall. Each collective is given slips of paper. Each collective has a different colour. Members of the collective are asked to write short phrases capturing things that their role is thinking or feeling immediately after the meeting with their father. They then fix their slips of paper around the image of their role. **C.** The exercise can be repeated but this time people are asked to write thoughts and feelings about their sisters at this moment. They will then fix those alongside the appropriate image.	**Recording thoughts and feelings. Interior monologues** The role on the wall strategy should result in a detailed colour-coded account of how the characters are feeling about themselves . . . **C.** and their sisters.
14.	**TiR/collective roles**	→ To encourage group members to start thinking about how they will use language to achieve their objectives	A brief strategy in which **TiR** as a court adviser says in turn to each of the collective roles, '*So Your Majesty, what are you going to say in your speech tomorrow?*'	

Activity	Drama strategy	Purpose	Teacher guidance	Opportunities for writing
5.	Writing in role	→ To further develop a key character → To give a clear purpose for persuasive writing	Cut up the words contained in the grid **(WR5, p. 163)** into separate one-word strips of paper placing the slips into three character-specific words boxes. Each collective role is given a word box containing only their characters' words. Using some of the words in the box they must now write the speech which they think their role would deliver at the ceremony tomorrow. **S.** We can make the task easier by saying that we'd like to see 'some' of the words in the box appear in the final speech or . . . **C. . . .** the task can become more challenging if we set a target for a specific number (say 10) of words to be included.	**Collaborative writing in role and persuasive writing (speech writing)** There are two possible approaches to this strategy and we might ask the collective roles to decide which one they think their character would use. **Approach 1** A daughter decides to write her own speech in which case this becomes a collective-role writing task **C. Approach 2** A daughter decides to bring in the best speech writers that money can buy. Here the group take on the MoE individual writers.
6.	Devising Soundtracks	→ To explore further the relationship between the four key characters in this drama using space and shape rather than language. → To provide material for the diary work in 19.	Working in groups of four, the task here is to devise the opening of the scene in which the King announces his decision to divide up his kingdom. The devised scenes must show the entrance of all four characters into a room where the ceremony is to take place and will finish with a freeze frame just as the King is about to start speaking. There will be no dialogue in this scene. When they enter the room all four characters know what the King is about to announce and the three daughters have already decided what they are going to say. Audiences watching these scenes will want to be clear about who is who, how the characters are feeling and how they feel about each other. Apart from their own bodies the only other resource which groups can use is a single chair. **C.** Put two groups together and ask the groups to create a soundtrack for their partner group's performance. Encourage groups to use found sounds, percussion, musical instruments rather than pre-recorded music.	

Activity	Drama strategy	Purpose	Teacher guidance	Opportunities for writing
17.	Performance	→ To evaluate different approaches to the movement brief and different interpretations of the characters and relationships	Place a chair at the centre of our working space and ask all group members to stand at the edges of the space in their groups of four. Each group must now decide where the door to 'their' royal room is. Now groups will show their work. After each performance we might want to discuss how groups signed character, whether or not we could recognize who was who and . **C.** . . . how the characters felt about each other and the event which was about to take place.	**Eye witness statement (writing in role)** Years later a member of the public or servant who watched the entrance of the royal family that day wrote down what he saw. The brief here is to create that account. **S.** The brief could be supported by supplying some opening words such as '*I can still see it now as if it was yesterday. The door opened and . . .*'
18.	Choral reading	→ To share the results of the speech writing work and to 'rehearse' the delivery of the speech at the up-coming ceremony	First the whole group needs to hear each of the speeches. Each of the three collectives must decide how their speech will be delivered. There are a number of options. **S.** They may decide to use a single voice throughout or to 'cut up' the speech between several readers. **C.** Alternatively they might use a choral approach with certain words emphasized or echoed by the whole group. Some of these approaches may need to be modelled or illustrated by teacher before the collectives make their decision. A rehearsal period will be needed before the three speeches are 'performed'.	
19.	TiR/collective roles	→ To offer a range of narrative options and to hand responsibility to the whole group for the development of the narrative	**TiR** as King Lear announces to the world his plan to divide up the kingdom. He invites each of his daughters to make their speeches. These can be delivered by a single reader or 'performed' using the choral approach devised in 18. After listening to the speeches the **TiR** will pause the action. The outcome will now depend on what the daughters have said in their speeches and the possibilities include: The three-way split is carried out as per the King's original plan. One or more of the daughters fails to please the King and he decides that not all of his daughters deserve their 'prize'. He changes his mind and decides to remain on the throne.	**Print journalism (Vox Pop)** Explain that newspapers and TV news programmes often print the views of ordinary people in the streets. These items are called Vox Pop; the voice of the people. **S.** (It might be useful to look at some recent press examples). Using **WR3B (p. 161)** as a template the task here is to create a range of appropriate comments from the streets.

Activity	Drama strategy	Purpose	Teacher guidance	Opportunities for writing
			You may want to break the scene and ask the class out of role to make a decision on this (see **Drama Strategies** for group decision strategies, e.g. **Voting with your feet**).	
20.	TiR/collective roles	→ To develop the narrative in line with the decisions made in 19	Restart the scene from the point of pause and use the **TiR** to bring it to a conclusion based on the group decision made in 19. Perhaps the **TiR** could sign with the words *'That is my final decision.'* Followed by an exit from the scene.	**Diary writing** Goneril, Regan and Cordelia each write a diary entry later that day. These diaries should be written individually and not as a piece of collaborative writing.
21.	Voice collage	→ This is an opportunity to turn fragments from the diary entries into an instant performance	So often as teachers we ask students not to talk when others are speaking and stress the importance of 'waiting your turn' during class discussions. Here's an opportunity to play with exactly the opposite. Ask each of the collectives to stand as a tight knit group. Start with Goneril and invite role members to read out fragments from their diary entries completely randomly. They shouldn't wait for others to finish in fact the effects can be much more powerful if we hear a chaotic collage of words. They can speak as many times as they wish and repeat phrases which they think might be particularly significant. Audience (the other two groups) may want to listen to these speech collages with their eyes shut. Repeat with Regan and Cordelia.	
22.	Improvisation	→ To consider the different ways in which stories end	Here group members can depart from collective whole-class drama and 'write' an ending of their own. It's important to discuss the ways in which stories end. Some stories give us a 'they-all-lived-happily-ever-after' ending (Cinderella) while others leave us in gloom and despair (Romeo and Juliet). Some stories end telling us everything we need to know (Shrek movies) while others leave us still wondering (Harry Potter). Soap operas never actually end at all as each episode sets up intrigue and tension for the next. Working in groups of four or five the brief now is to prepare a short improvisation which is set at some point in the future and which gives us a glimpse of an ending to this story.	

Activity	Drama strategy	Purpose	Teacher guidance	Opportunities for writing
23.	Performance		Now as these scenes are performed there will be multiple 'endings' to what has up to now been a whole group drama. There will be an opportunity to discuss why a specific group chose to ends the story in a particular way.	**Writing in role and letter writing** Invite class members to write a letter from any of the characters in this story. The letters need to be written 1 year, 5 years or 10 years after the division ceremony and can be written by one of the major characters or by a character we haven't specifically 'met' (e.g. servant, soldier, member of the Inner Chamber) or the eye witness who gave a statement in 18. Each letter will give us a glimpse of what happened based on one the ending which we have just seen. Remember a letter can't answer all the questions a reader might have. It can only give us a glimpse of the future.
24.	Script reading	→ To engage with Shakespearian text . → To compare Shakespeare's handling of character, theme and language with our own	If your class has been made aware that Shakespeare wrote a version of this story they may want to know how his turned out. **C.** In this scene the interest might be in comparing Shakespeare's skills as a speech writer with our own.	

UNIT 3
The Year of the Rats

Introduction

This unit is based on the legend of the Pied Piper of Hamelin. In the drama we are able to step into the famous story as members of a community under attack and question and challenge the decisions made by our leaders. Although the legend itself has a famous conclusion this drama may have a new ending based on the ideas and contributions of the participants.

Themes

→ Community

→ Honesty

→ Promises

→ Trust

→ Money

→ Greed

→ Vengeance

Writing opportunities

→ Advert copywriting

→ Photo captions

→ Audience Response Reports

→ Eye witness reports

→ Poetry

→ Headlines

→ Graffiti

→ Minutes of meeting

→ Writing to persuade and explain

→ Framing questions

→ Testimonials

→ Diary

→ Tweets

→ Structuring an argument

→ Alternative endings

Writing Resources (pp. 87–96)

→ Short story opening: The Grand Parade

→ Poem: *The Pied Piper*

→ Eye witness statement: rat attack

→ Template for writing minutes

→ Rat catcher poster

→ To whom it may concern: the Piper's testimonial

Other resources

Essential: Large sheets of paper (graffiti wall) marker pens
Optional: Drum

The Year of the Rats

Activity	Drama strategy	Purpose	Teacher guidance	Opportunities for writing
1.	**Teacher narration**	→ To establish a setting for the narrative	Explain that this drama will explore a famous story which has been told many times and in many ways. '*Although we may look some of the ways other writers have told this tale we are going to make a new version. Our own version. First we need to find out a little bit about the place where the story is set and meet some of the people who live there.*' Read 'The Grand Parade' **(WR1, p. 166).**	
2.	**Improvisation** **Mantle of the Expert (MoE)**	→ To establish a fictional location and functional roles for the whole class within that location	Split the class into seven sub-groups. Give each group a card stating one of the shop products mentioned in 'The Grand Parade' (hats, cakes, flowers, etc). Explain that they are going to become the people who own or work in that shop and that their shop is **the best of its kind in the whole city. Keep stressing that they are specialists in their field who sell only the very best.** Give the groups 10 minutes to 'set up' their shop. They can only use available chairs and tables and must imagine everything else negotiating where products are displayed and what roles in the business each of them has. Encourage them to set up their shop in role. Finally each shop must be given a name which is appropriate to its specialism. Ask one person from each group to write the chosen name on a large card and place it on the floor in front of the shop. **S.** Prior to naming the shops we might look at a range of real-life shops and discuss how well their names reflect the products which they sell.	**Advertisement copywriting** **S.** Examine some adverts for shops focussing on the language as well as the visual images used. The brief now is to write an advert for our own shop. This can be done as an individual or a collective group exercise.

Activity	Drama strategy	Purpose	Teacher guidance	Opportunities for writing
3.	**Teacher in Role (TiR)**	→ To validate and reinforce the shop locations created by the class → To model the role of wealthy shopper for the following activity	In role as a wealthy customer visit one of the shops. Ask to be shown round. Offer the shop owners the opportunity to describe a specific example of their merchandise. Ask questions which focus their attention but which allow them to invent and improvise, e.g. *I'm looking for a really spectacular cake for my daughter's wedding. What sort of things can you show me?'*	
4.	**Improvisation**	→ To share the invented shops with a wider group	Three of the groups will now become customers and visit the four remaining shops. The role of the customers is to make the shops feel 'real' and to find out as much as possible about the products on sale. After a couple of minutes freeze the improvisation and ask the customers what they have found, seen or bought. Now swap the groups over so that the shop keepers experience the role of customers.	
5.	**Still image**	→ To consolidate and share the ideas developed in 2, 3 and 4	Ask each of the shop groups to create a still image which sums up the atmosphere of their exclusive and highly successful shop. They can do this by representing shop workers, owners or customers. **C.** We might also want to offer the possibility of some of the group representing objects	
6.	**Teacher narration**		Read the first two verses of *The Piper* **(WR2, p. 167)**.	
7.	**Still image**	→ To examine human reactions to the sudden infestation by devising a single still image	The groups are now asked to make a second image of a moment when after the rats invade their shop. Stage the images one by one and discuss the ways in which the group have communicated feeling and narrative in a still image.	**Photo captions** **S.** Study some photo captions from newspapers. Discuss how caption writers have tried to use words to add meaning or impact to the photos. The brief now is to write captions for their own rat infestation images. The images can be re-staged with written captions placed in front or read aloud by a group member.
8.	**Image theatre**	→ To examine the contrast between the two images → To develop a movement/dance performance piece	Contrasts between the two images (5 and 7) can be discussed. Then groups work on a slow motion transition between the two images. **S.** You can use a drum beat to help groups cue and synchronize their movement transition.	

Activity	Drama strategy	Purpose	Teacher guidance	Opportunities for writing
9.	Performance carousel	→ To enable group members to watch and reflect on a range of group responses to the same task	The carousel starts with the groups standing in neutral (standing still arms at sides) in a large circle. You will decide which group will start and in which direction the carousel will turn (clockwise or anti-clockwise). You can cue the opening with the first beat of your drum. As each group completes its slow motion transition and freezes the next group will start. Each group can be paired with another group and asked to focus on their partner group's performance and remember what they have seen. They are told before watching, that they may need to share three things they liked about the scene/shapes and one thing that they wish to be improved.	**Audience Response Reports Reviews** The brief is to describe and evaluate the performance of the group with which they were paired: **S.** We may decide to provide a writing structure with prompts such as: → describe in writing the transition we have seen → write three things we liked about it → identify one thing that might improve it **C.** Alternatively the brief could be set without prompts.
10.	Statement prompts	→ To create a shared verbal account of the infestation	Ask the class to stand alone in a space. Explain that we are going to tell the story of the rats' arrival using just words this time. Ask them to think about the moment when they first noticed a rat. Move around the space and when you touch a person on the shoulder he must make a statement starting with the words *'The first thing I saw was . . .'* Repeat the exercise using other statement prompts such as → 'When I saw the first rat I . . .' → 'A rat looked straight at me and I felt . . .' → 'All I could hear was . . .'	**Eye witness reports (ordering events)** Use eye witness report forms **(WR3, p. 169)** to collect the details of a rat incident. Writers might choose to report on the attack in their shop or imagine a completely new incident which took place somewhere else in the city. **C.** Writers can use the details on the report to write a continuous prose account of an incident. This is an opportunity to discuss the structure and sequencing in reporting.
11.	Devising brief Sound collage (three variants)	→ To explore different ways of communicating a narrative using sound	Working in their shop groups class members create sound collages (or soundscapes) which communicate the horror of a rat invasion. Here are three suggestions for sound collages. **S.** 1. The first collage could be constructed by cutting and pasting fragments from the group member's eye-witness reports. **S.** 2. This work could then be repeated with the addition of live sound effects (screams, scratching claws, slammed doors, etc.) **C.** 3. Groups could make a collage which consists only of sound effects (no language allowed).	**Poetry writing (assembling sounds and images)** The writing brief is to use the collages as inspiration for short poems called, 'The Day the Rats Came'. Encourage writers to be experimental and abstract using fragments of sounds and phrases to give an impression of the event rather than a blow by blow report.

ctivity	Drama strategy	Purpose	Teacher guidance	Opportunities for writing
2.	**Performance**	→ To share and discuss the sound collage work	If they have made more than one sound collage groups can decide which one they perform to the whole group. Remember sound collages can be very powerfully experienced by audiences who have their eyes shut.	
3.	**Teacher narration**	→ To advance the narrative → To introduce a new character who can be questioned and challenged	Read verses 3, 4, 5 from *The Piper* **(WR2, p. 167)** or . . . . . . invite readers members of the class to read or . . . . . . tell the story in their own words. The important element here is the introduction of the Mayor and the anger of the people.	**Headlines** Using examples from some of the national tabloids examine with the class the way in which newspapers sensationalize events sometimes appearing to promote public outrage. Look at the language of exaggeration. For example, 'annoyance' becomes 'fury', 'irritation' becomes 'outrage', surprise becomes 'shock horror'. The task here is to write sensationalist headlines reporting the people's response to the rat infestation. **Graffiti** Sheets of paper are attached to the walls of the room and group members are invited to express (in role) their feelings about the infestation and the Mayor.
4.	**TiR**	→ To advance the narrative, build tension and provoke argument and protest	**TiR** as Hamelin's Mayor. The people of Hamelin have demanded a meeting with the Mayor. Group members can attend this meeting in role as either one of the shop owners or as another Hamelin resident. Stress that everybody attending the meeting is suffering directly from the rat infestation. The Mayor's role can be quite provocative insisting perhaps that the rat situation is only minor and suggesting that people are exaggerating. Ask the citizens to give specific examples of their rat experiences and be very sceptical. 'I can't believe that. Is that really true? And anyway what do you expect me to do about it?' You might even suggest that the people's hygiene standards might be responsible for the rat infestation.	**Minutes of meeting** Using the minutes of meeting template **(WR4)** the task is to write a brief account of an exchange between the Mayor and some of the citizens. **C.** Here is an opportunity to discuss reported speech (*The Mayor said that . . .*) or alternatively the template can be adapted so that direct speech is used (*The Mayor said . . .*)

Activity	Drama strategy	Purpose	Teacher guidance	Opportunities for writing
15.	MoE/designing in role	→ To provide an opportunity to work collaboratively in role to design a solution to the rat problem → To use language to pitch solutions to the Hamlin authorities	Present the rat catcher recruitment poster to the class **(WR5, p. 171)**. Organize the class into groups of 3 or 4 as teams of expert rat catchers. Explain that they are the best rat-catcher teams in the land. They are currently working on a new invention which they claim will eliminate rats immediately and effectively. Remember that this is a place where magic is practised and the inventions may make use of this. The brief for these teams of rat experts is to design their rat elimination device, write their pitch (see writing opportunity) and then to present their ideas to the Mayor. *NB: If the group is already familiar with the Pied Piper story we will need to point out that the piper in the story never applies for jobs. He just turns up. These are other rat experts.*	**Writing to persuade** This is a collaborative writing exercise. Having designed their device each time must write a short (1 minute maximum) presentation which is aimed to persuade the Mayor to buy their ideas. **Writing to explain** Another parallel writing opportunity here is to explain how the rat-catching device works.
16.	MoE/TiR	→ To share and evaluate the ideas of the design teams	As Mayor **(TiR)** invite each of the teams to present their short written pitches. Each team must decide how they will present the pitch. They might chose a single reader or . . . **C.** . . .read together chorally or . . . **C.** Use other team members to echo or emphasize certain words. When not presenting the other teams can revert to their previous roles as concerned citizens and help the Mayor to evaluate each presentation.	
17.	Teacher narration	→ To introduce the Piper into the story	*'The Mayor was just about to announce his decision on the Rat Catcher Team pitches when this happened'* . . . Read stanza 6 from *The Piper* **(WR2, p. 167)**.	**Eye witness accounts from three points of view** Working in groups of three each writer will describe the entry of the Piper from one of three perspectives: 1. the Mayor 2. one of the people 3. the Piper himself. Use stanza 6 from the poem *The Piper* as a description of the action but encourage writers to describe how their character felt as the event unfolded.

Activity	Drama strategy	Purpose	Teacher guidance	Opportunities for writing
18.	TiR	→ To prepare for the Piper's interview and to explore the language of effective questioning	**S.** As Mayor the objective of the **TiR** here is to encourage group members to think (in role as Hamelin citizens) about the questions they might ask the Piper at a formal interview. *'I can't make up my mind whether or not to trust him. What questions do we think we should ask him? What do we want to find out?* Some way needs to be found to list the suggested questions.	**Framing and prioritizing questions** Individually group members will select the questions which they think are the most important from the list gathered in the whole group session.
19.	TiR	→ To examine the Piper's experience and credentials	Here we will need to transfer our **TiR** and take on the role of the Piper. In role as the Mayor explain *'I don't have time to meet the Piper myself. I trust you as a group of citizens to interview the Piper for me and tell me if you think I should appoint him.'* The class will already have considered the questions which need to be asked. Out of role explain that you will now take on the role of the Piper. Sit the whole class together on one side of the room and place a single chair facing them. Start the **TiR** saying 'Thank you for agreeing to see me today. Shall I sit in this chair or would you prefer me to stand?' Tell our interviewers that you can give them a 100% guarantee that you will get rid of the rats. Explain that your methods involve a pipe but give no further detail. They will have to trust you. You are not prepared to negotiate on the payment. It's 100 gold coins or no deal. You may be prepared however to accept payment after the job is done. Show them the testimonial from The Piper **(WR6, p. 172)** and invite members of the interview committee to read it aloud. After a while thank the interviewers for their time and tell them that you will wait outside for their decision.	**Testimonial writing** Give the class copies of The Piper testimonial **(WR6, p. 172)**. In a leather bag the Piper carries many testimonials from other jobs that he has successfully completed all over the world. The task here is for each person to write a testimonial to place in the Piper's bag. The testimonials can be put together in a small book as a record of the Piper's extraordinary working life.
20.	**Storyboards/ performance carousel**	→ To create visual representations of the Piper's previous achievements	**C.** Having read the testimonials and working in small groups class members now devise a series of four still images which show one of the Piper's previous successes. Show these using a **performance carousel**.	

Activity	Drama strategy	Purpose	Teacher guidance	Opportunities for writing
21.	TiR	→ To advance the narrative	Explain out of role that *'the Mayor will be returning shortly to ask for your advice. Consider very carefully what you're going to tell him.'* Give the class an opportunity to discuss the issues alone before returning in **TiR** as the Mayor. The Mayor wants to be filled in on the interview. *'Tell me what he said. Did he give you any guarantees? Does he have any references or testimonials? Can we get him to do it for less money? So what do you think? Do we trust him? Do we use him or not?'* Thank your fellow citizens for their thoughtful advice and tell them that after thoughtful consideration you have decided to accept the Piper's offer. This decision may reflect the majority opinion or it may fly directly in the face of the advice offered. If there is opposition to the decision give people plenty opportunity to argue their case but stand firm.	**Writing in role: diary entry** The task here is to write a brief diary extract describing the interview and the final decision. **S.** Prompts. *What were you thinking and feeling when the Piper was being interviewed?* *What were you thinking and feeling when the Mayor made his decision?* **C.** Write a diary entry of the Piper describing his interview.
22.	**Teacher narration**		Read (or ask class members to read) verses 9 and 10 from *The Piper* **(WR2, p. 168)**.	**Writing in role: tweets** Citizens tweet friends outside the city describing the rats' departure in no more than 140 characters.
23.	**Still image** **Storyboard** **Devised** **movement**	→ To create a physical non-verbal representation of the rats' demise	**S.** In groups of five or six create a still image which shows a frozen moment from 9 and 10. **C.** Or create a movement piece which tells the story of the demise of the rats. **S.** The movement piece can start off as a storyboard which tells the story in a series of five still images. Groups then join the images together into a slow motion movement piece. Use a drum beat or find an appropriate recorded music to accompany this work (try *Time Lapse* by Michael Nyman).	
24.	TiR	→ To introduce a moral dilemma and develop tension	**TiR** as Mayor suggests to citizens that as the rats have now gone they may not need to pay the Piper. He may use a number of arguments, e.g. *The rats have gone so we don't have a problem any more. The money could be better spent on schools and hospitals. Maybe the rats would have gone anyway. What can he do if we all stand together and refuse to pay?*	

Activity	Drama strategy	Purpose	Teacher guidance	Opportunities for writing
25.	Conscience alley/ conscience forest	→ To set out an argument in a physical three-dimensional form and to evaluate its strengths and weaknesses through a formal ritual	The class is now invited to divide into two groups. Those who think that the piper should be paid on one side of the room and those who think he shouldn't on the other. The two groups form lines facing each other. In the first instance you in role as Mayor will walk slowly between the lines and as you pass by each person says something which will support his view. *NB. If a significant majority or even the whole group all take the same view then a conscience forest might be more effective strategy. Here individual group members stand in a space like trees in a forest and as the Mayor passes they express their argument.*	**Structuring an argument** Writers set out the argument which they have heard in two lists. 1. Pay. 2. Don't pay. Then they are asked to put the arguments in order of importance. This can be done by writing each argument on a different slip of paper and then experimenting with the ordering.
26.	Decision ritual **Voting with your feet**	→ To reach a group decision and to present that decision in a visual way	Group members are asked to walk to one of two places in the space. One will be labelled 'Pay' and the other 'Don't pay'.	
27.	Teacher narration	→ To advance the narrative towards a conclusion	Depending on the majority decision use one of the two following passages or better still write or improvise your own. **Either** *The Mayor looked at the Piper and said, 'The people wanted to pay you but I'm afraid the people don't understand complicated things like city finances. The people think that money grows on trees but these are difficult times and we can't just carry on spending. A hundred gold coins is a lot of money. Too much money to waste on a rat catcher. So I'm not paying. Not a penny. You hear me? Now get out of my office before I call the police.'*	**Alternative endings** People now write their own ending; the last page of the story. **S.** It might help to offer openings for these endings. E.g *1. The Mayor went home and poured himself a large glass of beer. He'd got rid of the rats and saved the city 100 pieces of gold. He felt very pleased with himself.* *2. The people were frightened now. Frightened that something bad would happen. Something really bad.* *3. The Piper sat on a hillside and angrily looked down at the City of Hamelin.*

Activity	Drama strategy	Purpose	Teacher guidance	Opportunities for writing
			The Piper gave the Mayor a long hard stare then slowly walked away.	
			Or	
			The Mayor looked at the Piper and said, 'It's the people's fault. I wanted to pay you but they had a vote and decided that the City couldn't afford the money. I told them. I said, "We've got to pay. We promised." But they wouldn't listen. What can I do? If it'd been down to me I'd have happily given you your money but they've made their decision so . . . I'm sorry. Shut the door on your way out will you?'	
			The Piper gave the Mayor a long hard stare and then slowly walked away.	

Having written their own endings our class may be interested in looking at other ways to conclude the story. The poem *The Piper* **(WR2, p. 168)** has two alternative endings and we may also want to look at Robert Browning's *The Pied Piper of Hamelin* or the version by the Brothers Grimm.

UNIT 4
The Lost Bag

Introduction

This unit provides an opportunity to explore a mystery/thriller narrative from inside the fiction. Class members take on roles as residents of a remote village. A bag belonging to a very important person has gone missing somewhere in the vicinity of this village. The authorities want it back. At any cost.

Themes

→ Communication

→ Freedom (of movement and speech)

→ Secrecy

→ Power and authority

→ Community

→ Trust

Writing opportunities

→ Pen portraits (self): Pen portraits (other)

→ Descriptive writing (imagined): descriptive writing (real life)

→ Flashback

→ Own version of story

→ Notes/lists/prioritization

→ Questions

→ Poetry: collaborative poetry writing

→ Headlines

→ Imagined first person narrative

→ Discursive writing

→ Writing for specific audience

→ Instructions/rules/legal document

→ For and against lists/persuasive writing

Writing Resources (pp. 97–107)

→ WR1: Village roles questionnaire

→ WR2: The Lost Bag

→ WR3: Lost poster

→ WR4: Instruction leaflet

→ WR5: Letter to all village residents

→ WR6: Travel information poster

→ WR7: Where do you stand?

Other resources

Essential: Sentence strips
Optional: Drum

The Lost Bag

Activity	Drama strategy	Purpose	Teacher guidance	Opportunities for writing
1.	Establishing roles	→ To give all members of the group an opportunity to devise a role within the community	The questionnaire **(WR1, p. 173)** may be a useful tool in establishing roles within a community. When inviting class members to invent personas for themselves there are several things which can cause problems later on. These can be easily avoided with some prompts and some clear guidance. First we need to explain that the drama we are starting takes place in a village quite a distance from the nearest town. Second we need to point out that to make this drama work we need to create 'ordinary' people who we might find in any normal village. With this in mind: a. Try to negotiate class members away from giving themselves very powerful roles, e.g. Village Mayor, Chairman of the Council, owner of all the land, etc. If very high status roles are needed they can emerge later in the drama. b. Avoid exotic characters. Football stars, drug smugglers and serving members of the SAS will not be useful characters in this particular drama. c. Explain that for this particular drama all group members need to take on the role of adults. Perhaps unsurprisingly when choosing a role for themselves children will often choose to be children! Participants will gain more if they engage with this particular drama from an adult perspective.	**Pen portraits (Self)** Writers are asked to link the questionnaire **(WR1, p. 173)** responses into a short piece of continuous writing Pen portrait (Other) Swap questionnaire details with a someone else and write a short pen portrait for our partner. Compare and discuss the two portraits. **C.** Descriptive writing (imagined) Add detail to the description from the bedroom window **(WR1, p. 173**) Consider time of day, light and weather conditions, sounds, people traffic passing. **Descriptive writing (real life)** Using the above as a model for a homework exercise describe what we can see from our real life bedroom window.

Activity	Drama strategy	Purpose	Teacher guidance	Opportunities for writing
			S. As teacher devise a village role for ourself. We could use this as a model to help class members start thinking about their own roles. A role here will also provide us with a Teacher in Role **(TiR)** character later on (see for example strategy 8).	
2.	**Mapping**	→ To establish a detailed location for this drama	Prepare for this by setting out a huge sheet of white paper (e.g. taped-together sections of sugar paper) on which you have drawn just the very basic geographical features of the village. It will be useful to include several routes in a main street, church and village hall. Leave the rest blank.	
3.	**Mapping in role** **Statement prompts**	→ To help class members engage with a fictional location from the perspective of an imagined role → To add geographical detail to the location	Tell the class members that the characters they have devised all live in this village. Using the last question in the questionnaire they must now identify their favourite places on the map and explain why they have chosen it. The places can be identified by: **S.** Teacher drawing or scribing the locations onto the map . . . **C.** . . .or by class members drawing their own symbols for the places on post-its and sticking them on one by one. A ritual can be set up as each class member adds their location saying 'This is my favourite place because . . .' A second mapping process can involve class members drawing their houses and placing those on the village map.	**Personal memory: writing in role** Ask the class to describe in writing a very brief memory of something that happened in the past in their chosen place. The memory explains why this a favourite place.
4.	**Teacher narration**	→ To introduce a narrative set in a location which the class have helped to create	Here we can either read the narrative opening **(WR2A, p. 174)** or write or improvise our own version. Either way it is important to include some of the geographical features and places supplied by class members in order to indicate that this developing story is theirs.	**Writing to describe. Writing in role** **S.** 'When I woke up and opened my curtains the village looked different . . .' Using the above as a prompt opening ask writers to describe what they saw and how they felt on the morning the posters went up. **C.** Set the writing task without the prompt.

Activity	Drama strategy	Purpose	Teacher guidance	Opportunities for writing
5.	**Reading in role**	→ To promote engagement with the narrative	Stick copies of the Lost poster **(WR3, p. 175)** all around the working space including some littering the floor. Ask the class (in role as village residents) not to speak as they pick up and read the posters.	
6.	**Statement prompts ('I wonder')**	→ To begin a questioning process which will underpin the narrative and develop tension	Sitting in a circle in role the villagers tell us what they are wondering at the moment when they first see the poster. In turn they share their thoughts with the wider group each starting with the words 'I wonder . . .' It's very useful to be able to record these 'I wonders' for later use.	**Notes/lists/prioritization** **S.** Ask people to repeat their 'I wonders' but this time to listen and make notes while they do. We will need to slow the pace of the process to give people time to record some of the statements. We can do this by cueing contributions with a drum beat. Stress that they won't have time to write complete sentences when making notes; *'sometimes we only need to jot down a word to remind ourself of a key idea.'* Now working in small groups they must use the notes to list as many 'I wonders' as they can and then from that list agree/negotiate the three 'I wonders' that they think are the most interesting.
7.	**TiR**	→ To increase tension and introduce the possibility of opposition to the actions of the authorities	A meeting is called. All the adult residents of the village are required to attend. The **TiR** (an official from the Ministry of Information) will start by distributing or displaying the instruction leaflet **(WR4, p. 176)** and then ask if anyone has any questions. A fairly stern tone is required here and the inevitable questions about the bag (*'What's in it? Who's is it? What makes you think it's here?'*, etc.) should be deflected with an arrogant *'That's not for us to know'* sort of answer. The only information that the **TiR** should reveal is that the bag is vitally important and that the authorities will do whatever it takes to get it back. The official is a very busy person and has to leave.	**C.** *There's an opportunity to point out here that writers particularly in adventure or thriller genres often make things get gradually worse before they get better. Easy solutions don't make for great stories.*

Activity	Drama strategy	Purpose	Teacher guidance	Opportunities for writing
			*NB. It is possible that somebody will announce that she has found the bag even producing a mimed version here at the meeting. Clearly the retrieval of the bag at this stage will put an abrupt end to the drama and so the **TiR** will simply say 'That's not the bag.' As the drama progresses some people will be very keen to 'find' the bag and solve the problem. When/if this happens the official must be called and she will always say 'That's not the bag.' The official might also issue warnings about future penalties for wasting Ministry time.*	
8.	**Working in role**	→ To ensure that the participants examine the instruction leaflet and consider some of its key implications	After the official has left the residents now have an opportunity to discuss what has just happened. As teacher we have two options. 1. **C.** We can leave them to it and just observe their responses to the situation or 2. **S.** We can join the discussion as a fellow resident using the role we devised for ourself in strategy 1. The most important function of this **TiR** would be to ensure that the villagers examine the instruction leaflet in detail and respond to its implications. *Hopefully at the end of this meeting there will be a number of questions and points which the villagers wished they'd raised when the official was present. If this is the case these points and questions can be listed and the official invited to return to the meeting.*	**Framing questions** **S.** Discuss the questions which were asked at the meeting. *Were our questions the right ones? Which were our best questions? What do we wished we'd asked? What makes a good question?* Writers now make lists of questions they wished they'd asked at the first meeting. Promise the group that if there are enough good questions we will ask the official to come back and face the village again.
9.	**Thought-tracking**	→ To express, audit and share the group members' responses to the developments	Ask the class to stand in a space. Narrate our way into the thought-tracking process by saying something like '*As the meeting closed the villagers were angry and confused. Something very strange was happening to them and their village.*' Ask them to think of a word or phrase that sums up how they felt at the end of the meeting. Walk around the space asking people to speak their chosen words as we tap them on the shoulder.	**Poetry writing** Ask the class to write their chosen words/phrases onto a sentence strip. Place the strips on the floor. Invite the class to tour the space with notebooks. They must write down what was on their own slip and then 'borrow' the words from five others. They then organize their collection of words and phrases to make a poem. On reading the results class members will hear their own words in the poems of others.

Activity	Drama strategy	Purpose	Teacher guidance	Opportunities for writing
10.	**Collective still image** **Choral reading**	➔ To find a physical expression for the mood of the village at this moment in the drama	Ask the class to stand in a circle round the edges of the space. One by one people will enter the space and adopt a still position making a shape which expresses what their role is feeling or thinking at the end of the meeting. Digital photographs from differing angles can be a good way of sharing the end result with the group. The exercise could be repeated with the thought-tracking words (see above) spoken as each group member enters the space. **C.** The poems written in strategy 9 can be turned into a choral performance. Working in small groups of four or five the class can experiment with weaving together their individual poems creating a choral piece in which words and phrases overlap, repeat and synchronize.	
11.	**Teacher narration**	➔ To advance the narrative and add tension	Ask the class to sit down and shut their eyes. Read from the narrative extracts **(WR2B, p. 174)** or write or improvise your own version.	
12.	**Working in role**	➔ To develop and explore a range of alternative narrative developments	In groups of three or four people are asked to discuss in role as a villager what might be in the bag. **S.** We might need to remind them that whatever is in the bag has to be important for the Ministry to go to all this trouble to retrieve it. Give the groups about 3 or 4 minutes to agree on a theory for the contents of the bag. They will need to describe their imagined contents in no more than ten words. *E.g. 'There's a massive bomb and the timer's ticking.'* Ask each group member to write down and learn the ten (or fewer) words which describe their theory for the content of the bag.	
13.	**Choral speaking**	➔ To share theories and alternative narratives	**'Live twitter':** First a member of each group will chose a member to read/recite their group's theory and the class will listen to the various theories. Stress that it's OK if two or more groups come up with the same theory. That's what happens in real life!!	**Print journalism. Headlines** Writers are asked to imagine that one of the theories we have heard is discovered to be true. The brief here is to create the headline and first lines of a newspaper story which reveals this information to the public

ctivity	Drama strategy	Purpose	Teacher guidance	Opportunities for writing
			'Twitter collage': Having listened to the various theories all class members are asked to walk slowly around the space repeating their own group's theory. A cacophony of sound will erupt and each participant will hear a distinct version of the collage.	**S.** It might be useful to examine the way real life newspapers have dealt with a recent event in their headlines and story openings. Stress to writers that it's OK to 'steal' some of the techniques and language used by the professionals.
			'Random twitter collage': A third variant of this strategy is to allow people to change theories as they walk around the space by borrowing somebody else's. This gives each participant a chance to articulate and evaluate other people's ideas and results in an ever-changing choral pattern.	
4.	**Teacher narration** **Reading in role**	→ To advance the narrative and increase dramatic tension	Ask the class to stand randomly in space and shut their eyes. Then place a copy of the letter **(WR5, p. 177)** on the floor in front of each person.* Read extract C from narrative extracts **(WR2C, p. 174)** then invite group members to pick up their letters and read. *Alternatively to save paper we might decide to display the letter on a white board.*	
5.	**TiR**	→ To gather testimony and to examine differing interpretations of recalled events	Announce a village meeting. Set out chairs in a meeting format, ask all class members to sit down in role and narrate: *'Everyone sat in silence. They were all thinking about what had happened when the soldiers came to their home. Many were very angry about the way in which the search was carried out. The soldiers who came to their houses were frightening and some damage was caused. There were rumours that some people had been hurt during the search. The official from the Ministry had agreed to attend the meeting to hear of their experiences and answer any questions but she looked a little nervous when she entered the room.* The **TiR** needs to be polite and grateful to villagers for their co-operation in the search operation. However she will suggest that any reports of damage or injury are exaggerations.	**Writing to describe and inform** Writers here are asked to describe the search of their homes. **S.** Writers might find some prompts useful, e.g. *What were the soldiers wearing?* *Did the soldiers say anything when they entered our home?* *What sounds could be heard as the search was carried out?* *How did we and our family feel during the search?* *Was anything broken or damaged?* *What happened after they'd gone?*

Activity	Drama strategy	Purpose	Teacher guidance	Opportunities for writing
15.	**Devising brief** **Movement/** **dance**	→ To communicate accounts of the search operation a physical non-verbal format	Working in groups of four or five the brief is to use details of the search accounts which we have heard at the meeting alongside the written accounts to create a short slow motion movement piece (no language allowed) called 'The Search'. Each piece should last no more than 30 seconds in performance. Set a clear time schedule and keep reminding the class of the time remaining before performance. The work could be accompanied by a slow drum beat or by recorded music accompaniment.	
16.	**Performance carousel**	→ To share ideas and to reflect on the way others have used the same resources to tell their stories	The carousel starts with the groups standing in neutral (standing still arms at sides) in a large circle. We will decide which group will start and in which direction the carousel will turn (clockwise or anti-clockwise). Use the music or drum beat to cue the opening. As each group completes its slow motion transition and freezes the next group will start.	**Performance review** The carousel is repeated and writer are asked to choose one of the performances to review. **C.** The task can be set without sub tasks . . . . . . or **S.** with the following prompt headings: a. Brief description of the performance b. Three things I liked about the performance c. One thing which might have improved the performance
17.	**Teacher narration**	→ To advance the narrative	Read from narrative extracts **(WR2D, p. 174)**	
18.	**Thinking in role**	→ To evaluate opposing viewpoints and clarify thinking	Identify two points at either sides of the working space as North and South and using chalk or strip of paper or string draw a line on the floor between the two. Explain that we are going to read out two statements expressed by different villagers **(WR7, p. 179)**. Start with the two statement A's. Read them very slowly and then display one at each end of the North/ South line. After listening to the statements and without speaking each person in their role as a villager must place themselves somewhere on that line. Explain that it's OK to be undecided and to place ourself somewhere in the middle.	**Discursive writing. Seeing both sides** **C.** Ask writers to take one of the opposing and interview members of the class asking them why they decided to stand where they did. The writer now has to set out his own reasons for taking a particular issue while acknowledging that others felt differently.

Activity	Drama strategy	Purpose	Teacher guidance	Opportunities for writing
			Alternatively we might partially agree with one of the statements in which case we would stand slightly closer to that end. Those who agree totally with the statement should obviously go to the end of the line. Repeat the process for statements B, C, D and E. **C.** We might decide to question or even challenge individuals about the reasons for choosing to stand in a particular position.	
19.	**In-role discussion** **TiR to support?**	→ To examine in role the dilemma faced by the community and to discuss possible responses	Explain that the community met once more to discuss what they should do. **S.** We might again choose to support this strategy in role ourself as a fellow villager. The reason for doing this would be to informally chair the meeting ensuring that participation is evenly shared and that everybody has a chance to have their say. **C.** Alternatively we might leave our class to conduct the discussion without our in role presence offering our observations later.	
20.	**TiR** **Writing in role**	→ To retell the story to an outsider	The idea of making some covert contact with the outside world might well come out of the meeting held in strategy 19. If so use this opportunity. If not explain in a **TiR** as villager that someone has agreed to attempt to get out of the village tonight under the cover of darkness. That person will take letters written by villagers and post them when she gets to the nearest town. The messenger is about to leave. Explain that villagers have just half an hour to write a letter to someone outside the village. It could be to a friend or relative or it could be to a newspaper. Either way. This could be their only chance to let the outside world know what's been going on. *NB. Should any villager think that writing a letter is too dangerous he can choose to write a diary entry instead.*	**Writing in role. First person narrative (writing for specific audience)** **S.** In asking class members to write their letters they need to bear the following in mind: 1. Who are we writing to? 2. What do we want the person who receives the letter to think/feel/do about our situation? 3. We don't have much time. The letters need to be brief and to the point.

Activity	Drama strategy	Purpose	Teacher guidance	Opportunities for writing
21.	Ritual	→ To formalize the sending of the letters and to share fragments of their contents	When the letters are finished ask people to choose a tiny fragment from their letters; a sentence or phrase which they think is the most important bit of their letter. Put a large envelope on a table in the centre of the room. Ask group members one by one come to the table and speak the words they have chosen as they place their letters inside the envelope.	
22.	TiR	→ To introduce an unexpected narrative development which will present the group with a complex dilemma requiring some discussion and a difficult decision	As soon as the letters have been placed in the envelope return in **TiR** as the official from the Ministry. You have asked to speak to the whole village as there has been an important development. Adopt a more conciliatory role this time. Explain that the bag has been found and that all travel and communication restrictions have been lifted. Invite questions. Explain that the bag was found in another village some 10 miles away and that the problem is now resolved. Apologise for any inconvenience caused and thank the villagers for their co-operation. Offer them substantial financial compensation which will be payable as long as they agree never to talk of this incident. Each family will receive a sum of £5,000 if they agree to sign a 'silence agreement'. If any member of the community breaks that silence agreement the money will be taken back from everybody. Leave the meeting telling them that they have 1 hour to agree.	*There's an opportunity here to talk about the unexpected as a narrative device in fiction. How does an unexpected plot development make us feel?* **C. Instructions/rules/legal document** Using the instruction leaflet **(WR 4)** as a template and working in groups of three, class members must write a version of the document which the villagers are going to be asked to sign. The instructions and rules (and the consequences of failing to obey them) must be very clear.
23.	Working in role TiR	→ To air two sides of an argument and to set out the key points	The **TiR** as one of the villagers needs to hold back and provide sufficient counterarguments to ensure that the decision facing the community is explored from several angles. If the prevailing view is that we accept the money and sign the silence agreement then the **TiR** might remind the villagers of how they felt when the Ministry limited their freedom adding perhaps that the world should know about this.	

ctivity	Drama strategy	Purpose	Teacher guidance	Opportunities for writing
			If on the other hand the view is that the letters should be sent and the Ministry's offer rejected then the **TiR** should remind the villagers that a spurned Ministry might turn nasty and also argue the advantages of taking the money! **If the group is evenly divided and are effectively arguing these points the TiR needs to do nothing!**	
4.	**Decision alley**	→ To audit the consensus in the group and to examine the respective strengths of two opposing arguments	Members of the class are asked to join one of two opposing viewpoints. a. Sign the agreement, accept the money, keep quiet about the lost bag affair. b. Tell the Ministry to get lost and tell the world what's happened. Each person must choose a few words which he thinks will persuade a neutral person of their viewpoint. The opposing viewpoints form two lines facing each other and you in **TiR** as villager who can't decide walk slowly through the 'alley'. As you pass villagers will loudly whisper their persuasive phrases. You can adjudicate at the end or tell the group that it's so hard to decide you need help. Invite others to experience the 'alley' for themselves. If this strategy reaches a decision this could form the end of the drama. Below however are some suggestions for further development of this work.	**For and against lists** The arguments from both sides of the 'alley' can be listed and then turned into a piece of discursive writing in which both sides of the argument are set out in a balanced way. **S.** *Useful linking words and phrases here could be offered such as 'however' . . . 'on the other hand' . . . 'other people say that' . . .* **C.** Alternatively the arguments from only one side of the list can be used to make a piece of persuasive writing which advances only one decision and course of action.

5. Alternative developments of the drama

1. Instead of the arrival of the official from the Ministry in **strategy 22** you could use your villager **TiR** to confess to the group that you found the bag a week ago and were too scared to tell anyone. The bag is hidden under the floorboards in your house. You're really scared and you don't know what to do. You are now asking for their advice and help. Here a completely different discussion can take place. Perhaps you can offer to wait outside the meeting while the villagers decide what to do with you. It's possible that they may need a decision alley here which may bring the drama to a completely different ending. If for example the village decides to protect the **TiR** and continue to conceal the bag the narrative may well continue.

2. At the end of **strategy 21** after the villagers have placed their letters in the envelope ask group members to stand in a circle and close their eyes. When they have shut their eyes place a bag** in the middle of the space. Narrate that *the letters were sent in the night and in the morning when they woke up the Villagers saw something odd in the middle of the village square* (or some other central vantage point on our map). When they open their eyes and see the bag they now have a number of questions to ask and decisions to make all of which could lead to further developments for this drama.

***If you decide to use this approach you might want to insert a photograph of the bag you are going to use in the poster (WR3, p. 175). It's a powerful experience for group members to be able to finally see and touch an object which has only existed in their imaginations.*

UNIT 5
Lorry

Introduction

Using fictional, non-specific national boundaries this unit explores the migrant experience and helps us to empathize with those who have taken enormous risks to move from their homelands.

Themes

- → Home
- → Travel
- → Nationhood

- → Safety
- → Separation
- → Hope

Writing opportunities

- → Interview
- → Poem
- → Character study/pen portrait
- → Lists
- → Letter (in role)
- → Poem. Shared writing
- → Audience Response Report. Writing to describe

- → First person narrative (in role)
- → Play script stage
- → Play script radio
- → Note taking
- → Caption
- → Advertising copy
- → Diary (in role)

Writing Resources (pp. 180–4)

- → WR1: A message to the World
- → WR2: A message to the World
- → WR3: The People Smuggler

- → WR4: A letter found on a kitchen table
- → WR5: Lorry poem (version 1)
- → WR6: Lorry poem (version 2)

Other resources

Essential: Sentence slips
Optional: Torch, drum, digital camera

The suggested statements and prompts in this unit are available for download from the companion website.

Lorry

Activity	Drama strategy	Purpose	Teacher guidance	Opportunities for writing
4.	'Move if . . .'	→ To introduce some of the themes of this drama → To begin to promote empathy for the roles we are going to encounter by recalling relevant experiences of our own	Ask the class to stand in a circle. The instruction for this activity is very simple. As teacher you are going to make a series of statements. Members of the class must slowly walk across the circle and take up a different position if the statement applies to them. **S.** If we are using this strategy for the first time with a group it's a good idea to model it with a couple of very straightforward statements which are likely to apply to a large number of people. For example, *Move if you're wearing black shoes*. Or move if *your birthday is in a month starting with the letter J.* You should cross the circle if the statement applies to you. The statements for this drama could include ***Move if . . .*** *. . . you've ever gone on a journey that lasted longer than six hours* *. . . you've been on a journey that lasted longer than a day* *. . . you've ever lived in another country* *. . . you've ever visited a country where you didn't speak the language* *. . . you've ever said goodbye to someone not knowing if you'd ever see them again* *. . . you wish you had more money* *. . . you wish you lived in a bigger house* *. . . you'd like to live in another country one day*	**Interview, note-taking and reporting** Working in pairs pupils in turn interview their partners about one of the times in this exercise when they moved. The brief here is to get as much information as possible from our partner about the occasion in question. Allow 5 minutes for each interview and when both are complete give interviewers a further 10 minutes to write up their notes into a brief report which captures the key information.

Activity	Drama strategy	Purpose	Teacher guidance	Opportunities for writing
2.	**Still image (statues) #1**	To experiment with ways to communicate complex ideas through gesture and shape	Read the extract from the Emma Lazarus poem **(WR1, p. 180)** and ask the class to imagine that other countries have used these words on statues at ports and airports. Discuss what the poem is saying. Working in groups of three or four ask the class to use their bodies to make other statues on which this poem has been engraved. **S.** Support this work by suggesting that groups select six words from the extract which they think are very important. They can try to express these words their chosen words in their new statues. We might suggest that 'tired' could be a useful word when making a statue and invite other suggestions.	
3.	**Still image (statues) #2**	→ To repeat the statue experiments with a contrasting message	Ask group members to study the words on the sign in Arizona **(WR2, p. 180)**. In the same groups now make a statue which might have been put up to make the message even clearer. **S.** Again we might want to support this activity with a word selection process.	**Poetry** The task here is to turn the message on the Arizona signpost into a very short poem. The poem expresses the feelings of someone reading the sign. Writers can use up to five words from the sign in their poem. **C.** Alternatively the task can be set from the point of view of the person who put up the sign.
4.	**Performance**	→ To share and evaluate ideas	Here class members are able to observe and discuss the work of others. As well as learning to observe and reflect people are also practicing audience skills. Starting with the statues made in strategy 2 call half of the small groups X and the other Y. First the X groups will show their statues at an exhibition while the Y groups become audience. Reassure statues that they will only have to hold their positions for about 30 seconds. Invite audience members to wander around the space and study the statues in total silence looking out for things which they find interesting. Once the statues have relaxed and returned to neutral the audience members can report back. Statues or pieces of statue which visitors want to comment on can be reconstructed to illustrate the points being made. The groups then swap over with visitors becoming statues and vice versa. The process can be repeated with the statues based on **WR2 (p. 180)** from Activity 3.	

tivity	Drama strategy	Purpose	Teacher guidance	Opportunities for writing
	Teacher in role (TiR)	→ To launch the narrative of this drama and to pace the participants directly in role	Ask the class to sit on the floor facing us. Explain that you are going to take on a role by reading an extract from a play **(WR2, p. 180)**. *Alternatively you might prefer to improvise the role without direct reference to the text.* Explain that if they listen carefully a picture will start to emerge of who they are and what they are doing here in this place today. See if they can imagine what the speaker looks like and how we feel about him. When they are still and ready read the extract.	**Character study/pen portrait (first draft)** **S.** Ask group members to jot down their thoughts about the People Smuggler using the following prompts *What did he look like?* *What sort of things did he say?* *How did I feel about the things he said?* *How did I feel about him?* **C.** Set the same task without the prompts.
	Collective role/ TiR	→ To promote engagement with the drama → To evaluate how well the group is understanding and engaging with the role	The groups are now going to take on a collective role. (For guidance on setting collective roles, see **Drama Strategies**.) Together the whole class is going to become the People Smuggler. Explain that you are now going to change roles. The meeting has just finished. The travellers have gone home to get ready for the journey but one of them **(TiR)** has stayed behind. He has a question for the People Smuggler. This is a very low status role. The traveller is very nervous about speaking to the smuggler. You want to know if you can bring some extra luggage. You were hoping to bring three or four bags; would that be OK? If your request is turned down try respectfully and perhaps nervously challenging the smuggler. *'That doesn't seem fair . . . surely you can make an exception for me . . . what difference will a couple of cases make? etc.* In the unlikely event of the smuggler agreeing to your request ask for more concessions.	**Character study/pen portrait (second draft)** Having now been part of the collective role as the People Smuggler writers are offered the chance to go back to their pen portraits and see if there's anything they'd like to add or change. **C.** A more challenging task might be to rewrite the portrait in the first person. **Lists** Ask your writers to imagine that they are about to start packing for the journey and, bearing in mind the very restricted space available, they must make a list of things they are going to pack. Ask them to try and stay in role as travellers while they write.
	Teacher narration **Thought-tracking (Statement Prompts)**	→ To examine the narrative from the point of view of just one of the travellers → To provide a stimulus and a model for the writing of letters	Read the letter found on a kitchen table **(WR4, p. 182)**. (We might feel that the class doesn't need an exemplar letter. It could be argued that the exemplar might limit writers' imaginations tempting people to produce something very similar to the original.) If using the letter explain that this letter was written by a 16-year-old boy and that it was just one of many other letters written that night.	**Letter (writing in role)** Each member of the class in role as a traveller is asked to write their own letter to a person or people who they are leaving behind. It may be that the journey has been discussed many times before or it might have been kept secret as in the example letter.

Activity	Drama strategy	Purpose	Teacher guidance	Opportunities for writing
			S. Before starting work on their letters it might be useful to hold a thought-tracking ritual. Ask the group to sit randomly in a space and shut their eyes. Ask them to imagine themselves back in the role of a traveller and think of one of the reasons why we are about to go on this difficult and dangerous journey. Give the group a minute's silent thinking time and then in their own time they can open their eyes, stand up and speak a sentence starting with the words **'I'm leaving tomorrow because . . .'**	
8.		→ To share the letters and some fragments of the travellers' back stories	**Exhibition** Ask group members to find a space and to put down their letters on the floor. Group members now become visitors to reading gallery and move around the space reading letters. They can be asked to remember one thing which they read which interested them. These can be shared in a reflection/discussion session afterwards.	
9.	**Choral reading**	→ To examine ways in which written text can be re-structured and new meanings made	Working in groups of five or six members each group member now chooses a phrase or brief sentence from his letter. These phrases are then written down on slips of paper. The groups then try out different ways of reading their phrases and then compose choral performances based on their experiments **S.** If our class is new to this sort of work we might suggest or even model some of the techniques which could be used including perhaps repetition, echoes, volume levels (whispering through to shouting), choral effects such as single voice/whole group in unison, singing or voice distortion. Suggest also that the performers could decide to move around when presenting their work so that sound sources are constantly changing.	**Poetry writing and shared writing** Using only words and fragments from their letters groups work together to create an abstract poem called 'Goodbye'.
10.	**Performance**	→ To share and reflect on the devised choral pieces	Audiences can be asked to listen to these choral performances with their eyes shut. This sometimes intensifies the dramatic impact but can also lessen performer inhibition!	**C. Audience Response Report, writing to describe** The writing brief here is to describe as vividly as we can the experience of hearing one of the performances.

Activity	Drama strategy	Purpose	Teacher guidance	Opportunities for writing
1.	**Improvisation (movement)**	→ To move the narrative on → To promote engagement with role	Ask the class to stand at the edges of the space. It is morning. Today the journey will begin. One by one people will walk into the space and arrive at the pick up point carrying their single suitcases. Then they sit or stand and wait. Nobody speaks. Ask people to try to think how they are feeling and what they are thinking.	
2.	**Thought-tracking (statement prompts)**	→ To share and reflect on different perspectives of the same event	When everyone has entered the space allow a few moments of stillness before asking the class to go back to the edges of the space. Now repeat the process but this time each arrival will speak a line as they enter the space. **S.** The work of the class can be structured and focussed here through the use of statement prompts such as . **'Right now I'm feeling . . .'** Variants could be: **'I'm leaving tomorrow because . . .'** (a repeat of the reasons given in strategy 7) **'The most important thing I've put in my case is . . .'** **'The thing I feel most sad to leave behind is . . .'**	**Writing in role (first person narrative)** Group members must write a first person present continuous monologue which starts with the words. *'It's early in the morning. It's still dark I'm standing in a car park holding a little suitcase. I'm waiting for a lorry . . .'* **S.** Useful prompt phrases might be *'I can see . . .'* *'I'm feeling . . .'* *I'm thinking . . .'*
3.	**Improvisation/ devising brief**	→ To advance the multiple narratives → To consider the best way to structure and to stage their ideas to create maximum impact for audience	Working in teams of four group members must start by repeating for each other the reason which they gave for leaving in the previous phase of the drama. The group must now choose one of those reasons to develop into a short piece of performance called *The Last Straw*. The brief is to create a short (30 seconds max) scene depicting an incident . . . something that happened that finally made that person decide that he really had to leave. Lots of other incidents may have preceded this one but this was 'the last straw'. The scenes should involve all four 'actors'. Dialogue can be developed through improvisation and experimentation should be encouraged but enough time	**Play script (stage)** **S.** *Before starting this work it's a good idea to look at some published play scripts to see how they are set out.* Writers now turn their devised scene into a play script. Here is an opportunity to 'improve' on some of the lines and make the scene more effective. Alternatively writers might conclude that the original unscripted version worked better and decide to simply record that. **Play script (radio)** **C.** The same exercise but this time we are writing for radio. An opportunity to listen to some radio drama and examine how writers use sound effects as well as dialogue to tell stories.

Activity	Drama strategy	Purpose	Teacher guidance	Opportunities for writing
			should be given to rehearse the scene so that it is relatively 'fixed' by performance time.

While devising their scene group members need at the same time to be acutely aware of their audience, i.e. to be thinking like directors as well as actors.

S. We can help them by asking them:

'where in this whole space are you going to perform this?'

'where will you place the audience?'

'check out what it will look like from there?'

'are you sure that the audience will see and hear exactly what you want them to?' | |
| 14. | Performance | → To share and evaluate ideas both in terms of content and staging | Remind the performers of the importance of sight-lines and the positioning of audience. Ask the audience to listen and watch very carefully. Tell the audience that they are going to be asked to choose one of the pieces to evaluate in writing and that there are going to be two performances of each piece

First performance

Here the audience just watches and listens as carefully as they can. At the end of these performances audience members must decide which one they are going to write about.

Second performance

Audience members have a chance to see their chosen piece again and this time to take notes. If we are going to use an audience response structure format it would be useful to give this out prior to the second show. | **Note-taking**

By the time the second performances come round the audience members will have decided which piece they are going to write about. The pieces are very brief so here is an opportunity to discuss methods of recording things at speed.

Audience Response Reports

Response Reports need to describe and evaluate the performance in a constructive way.

S. A prompt format can help this. For example, in this case

1. Describe the scene so that someone who hadn't seen it could imagine it clearly.

2. Did the incident we saw (the last straw) clearly explain why the person had to leave?

3. Write down three things we particularly liked about the scene.

4. Can we think of one thing that might have improved it?

C. An additional brief might be to focus on the staging asking writers to describe and evaluate the way a group has used space, shape and proxemics. |

ctivity	Drama strategy	Purpose	Teacher guidance	Opportunities for writing
5.	**Teacher narration**	→ To advance the narrative and develop dramatic tension	Ask the class to imagine that that many years later one of the people who was on that lorry wrote this poem. Read the poem **(WR5, p. 183)**.	
6.	**Storyboarding**	→ To examine a part of the text in detail and reinterpret it in a single image	Divide the group into eight subgroups. Allocate to each group a verse from the poem. (They will need paper copies at least of their own verse.) The brief is to capture that verse in a single still image using just their bodies. Allow just 5 minutes for the design of the images. Ask the class to stand at the edges of the space. Present the storyboard by slowly re-reading the poem. As each verse begins the relevant group walks into the space and slowly forms their image withdrawing to the edge of the space as the next verse starts. Digital photos of each of the images can provide a detailed record of the storyboard. **C.** In addition we can: → Show the storyboard without the poem. → Invite each subgroup to direct the whole group to join in with their shape so that we now have a whole group storyboard.	**Caption writing** Writers are asked individually or in teams to write captions to place under each of the images. (Photos make this work easier.) We can impose creative constraints here, e.g. setting a word limit for each caption. (Single word captions can be very effective!)
7.	**Mantle of the Expert (MoE)**	→ To reinterpret a text for a specific audience	Read Lorry version 2 **(WR6, p. 184)**. Explain that this is the text of a children's picture book for children under 7 which tells the same story. In groups of four as expert children's book illustrators the brief is to design the images for the picture book using just their own bodies and found objects. The groups will need to study the text and decide how images are needed. **C.** Having devised the images groups can devise a way to show book will be 'read' in performance. How will the group manage the transition between the images; the turning of the pages of the picture book?	**Copy-writing: advertisement for a children's book** **C.** Writers here need to look at how the publishing industry advertises new products and discuss the language and imagery of book promotion. The task here is to write a newspaper advert announcing the publication of 'Lorry'; a new picture book for under 7's. In creating their copy writers may need to ask if they are appealing to children or their parents?

Activity	Drama strategy	Purpose	Teacher guidance	Opportunities for writing
18.	**Thought-tracking**	→ To promote empathy by 'experiencing' in role a moment of tension from the poem	Use chairs or blocks to create the inside of the lorry and ask the group members to enter this space in role. Read verses 5 and 6 from Lorry version 1 **(WR5).** A black-out or partial black-out could make the following thought-tracking activity more compelling and dramatic although some teachers may be concerned that this could alarm younger children. The thoughts of the 'Travellers' as the Lorry is searched are activated by a torch beam. As the beam crosses any part of their bodies the 'Travellers' repeat their brief thought or feeling. Rapid movement of the torch can create a loud collage of simultaneously expressed thoughts while a still beam will activate a single voice. Turning the torch off or shining it at the ceiling will result in silence.	
19.	**Ritual**	→ To begin the process of 'writing' conclusions to the individual narratives	The strategy here will hopefully offer a wide range of possibilities. Ask the class to resume their positions from the previous strategy and announce that the lorry has now arrived at its destination. The doors are about to open and group members must imagine what's outside. Remind the group that when the journey in the poem is over the writer notices smells (bread) and strange sounds (sea gulls) but that each group member can decide what's outside for them. **S.** We might want to make this clearer by saying something like. *'We don't have to find the same thing that the writer found and we don't have to find the same things as each other. This is not a collective role so it doesn't matter if one Traveller gets out and finds a busy city street whilst another finds an empty beach. What you find when the door opens might be a delight or it might be a disappointment. It's up to you.'*	**Sensory list** Writers list the things they notice with their senses during first minute after the lorry doors opened. **S.** *'A minute is quite a long time. In a new strange place the light and the weather might be unfamiliar and you would be bombarded by new sights, sounds and smells. Just make a list of all the things you notice.'* **First person narrative: writing to describe** Writers now turn their lists into a piece of descriptive prose . . . **S.** . . . starting with the words: *'At last the doors opened and I climbed out into daylight.'*

Activity	Drama strategy	Purpose	Teacher guidance	Opportunities for writing
			Give people a few minutes to decide what it is they're going to see, hear and smell when the doors open. Use a drum beat for each group member to emerge. As they step out of the shape each person will tell something that they can see. We can repeat the ritual for sounds and smells and feelings.	
20.			**Resolution/multiple endings** Explain that this story like all migration stories has a different ending for each traveller. Some will have found what they were looking for while some will have been disappointed. Some will eventually find their way back home while others will make a new home in a new place. There will be happy endings and sad ones.	**Diary entry/writing in role** The task here is to write a diary entry written by our traveller role some years in the future. It's just an account of an ordinary day in that person's life but when we have read it we will know if the journey in the lorry was worth it or not.

UNIT 6
When the Bees Died

Introduction

This drama takes us into a future where the honey bee has become extinct. Participants will grapple with life in an uncertain world of food shortages, public unrest and economic crisis. In role they will be required to make difficult personal and public decisions and face moral dilemmas particularly when it transpires that there is a remote corner of the world where the honey bee has survived.

Themes

→ Food

→ The environment

→ Fairness

→ Honesty

→ Power

→ Wealth

Writing opportunities

→ Menu: writing to describe

→ Editing and rewriting (writing to inform)

→ Diary

→ Play script

→ Letter

→ Chants and slogans

→ Eye witness account (writing to describe)

→ Caption

→ Evaluation

→ Press release (writing to explain)

→ First person narrative (writing to describe and inform)

→ Speech bubbles

→ Letter (writing to persuade)

→ Extract from history book

Writing Resources (pp. 185–91)

→ WR1: Shopping lists

→ WR2: Public Statement. Ministry of Information

→ WR3: Public Information Leaflet. Ministry of Information

→ WR4: School lunch menu 2024

→ WR5: World War Two rationing poster

→ WR6: Say 'no' poster

→ WR7: Item on radio and TV news

Other resources

Essential: Placard making materials (large sheets of paper, cardboard, paints, marker pens)
Optional: Drum, digital camera

When the Bees Died

Activity	Drama strategy	Purpose	Teacher guidance	Opportunities for writing
1.	**Vocal warm-up**	→ To establish focus and concentration → To identify some of our favourite food items (this will help to emphasize the impact of 'losing' of these items later in the drama)	Standing alone and randomly around the space ask the class to think about food. Ask people to choose three things that they most like to eat. Walk briskly round the space and ask people to speak one of their items as we pass them. When you call 'change' they must swap to a different item from their chosen three. Call change a second time and hear the third item as we pass. Now invite group members to move about the space quietly repeating one of their chosen food words. If they meet others who are saying the same word they must form a group and move together. After a while freeze the activity. **C.** See if any groups have formed up and discuss the effect that this might have had on where people are now standing and on the rhythms and sounds which we heard.	**Menus: writing to describe** Look at restaurant menus and food adverts. Examine the ways in which writers use language to 'big-up' flavours, textures and ingredients to make our mouths water. The task here in small groups is to take some of the food items which they chose in the warm-up exercise and describe them in this way. **S.** We might first want to create a bank of useful adjectives.
2.	**Discussion**	→ To introduce and discuss the collapse of the honeybee population and the impact which many experts believe this would have on the world's food production	It is important to remind your group that although the drama we are going to start is a fiction there are real life concerns that honeybees are in danger. **S.** In some classes we will need to explain the basics of pollination and why the demise of the honeybee could have such an impact on food production. Ask the group to imagine a world in say 10 years time when all the honeybees have died and show them **WR1 (p. 185)** explaining that this is what many experts believe that our food options might look like in such a world. Discuss how group members would feel about such a change in diet.	

Activity	Drama strategy	Purpose	Teacher guidance	Opportunities for writing
3.	**Teacher in Role (TiR)** **Mantle of the Expert (MoE)**	→ To 'enter' the drama and start to examine some of the key issues from within a fiction → To take on imagined skills and responsibilities and to use those skills and responsibilities to carry out specific tasks	It is now 2023 and the honeybees have all died. The **TiR** here is that of the Minister of Food. He has recruited a group of special advisers. You might decide to use your role to hand on the MoE to the group saying something like. . . . *'Thank you for coming to this emergency meeting. Yet again I am going to need your skills and knowledge. Many times in the past you have helped the government. In the great droughts you advised us how to save water. When the wheat crops failed you showed us how to feed our people using other food sources. I know that you are very wise I am confident that you people will help me to avoid making mistakes in the current crisis.'* Tell the advisers that you have written a statement and you want them to look at it before it goes public. Show them **WR2 (p. 186)** and tell them that you're worried about the impact that this announcement might have. *'People might start panic buying. There could be violence. I have to tell people something but is this the right statement? I'm really not sure.'* Explain your fears and worries to our advisers and then divide participants into subgroups with the brief to improve the statement. **See writing opportunity.**	**Editing and rewriting (writing to inform)** Working in small groups the task here is to edit or rewrite the Minister statement to ensure that there is litt or no panic in the country. **Writing to inform (for a specific audience)** **C.** An additional task could be to write a statement on the food situation which is aimed specifically at young children.
4.	**Writing in role** **Reading in role** **Teacher narration**		When the suggested editorial changes come in reconvene the advisory group and ask representatives from each group to read their amended statements. In the light of these you might decide to make adjustments to the original statement. At the end of the session you need to teacher narrate *'That night the statement was read out on TV and radio. It was heard in every home in the land.'*	

Activity	Drama strategy	Purpose	Teacher guidance	Opportunities for writing
5.	**Still images**	→ To introduce a second role so that class members can experience the drama from both public and domestic perspectives	Now the smaller groups formed earlier need to become family groups. Groups need to cast their families. With this drama its probably useful to impose constraints about age for example *'no very small children or babies. Everybody in this family is old enough to read the statement.'* The family has just received the statement from the Ministry of Food. Ask each group member to imagine how their character would feel on hearing this announcement. **S.** We might suggest options such as fear, concern, anger, confusion, sadness, panic, reassurance. The brief now is to make a still image of the family just after reading or hearing the statement. The image should give us an idea of what each family member is thinking. One by one these still images can be examined and discussed by the wider group.	**Diaries** We're going to imagine that each family member keeps a diary. The writing task is to write a passage from a diary entry which covers the moment when the announcement was made. **S.** An opening sentence might provide a prompt for some writers. *'We switched on just in time for the news and there it was . . . the announcement.'*
6.	**Thought-tracking**	→ To share individual responses to the developing story	Groups now 'reassemble' their family images with group members entering the image one at a time. As each person enters the image she briefly states what her role is thinking. These thought-tracked images can be shown to the wider group as mini performances	
7.	**Improvisation**	→ To develop family roles and further explore the implications of the food crisis at a domestic level	Starting with the still image each group is now asked to improvise a very brief scene which gives us a glimpse of how this family might be affected by the crisis. The scenes need to finish with a still image. Groups could decide to return to the starting image or create a new one.	**Play scripts** Working together in their family groups writers are going to try turn their improvised family scene into a play script. If while they are writing they think of better lines than the ones used in the improvisation then it's fine to make changes. **S.** It may be necessary to look at some play scripts and see how writers have set them out (several formats are used). **C.** Some playwrights provide lots of stage directions while others including Shakespeare offer hardly any. An additional task for some groups might be to include stage directions in their scripts. Remember that these directions are written to help actors and directors but they may also make important meanings for audiences.

Activity	Drama strategy	Purpose	Teacher guidance	Opportunities for writing
8.	TiR MoE	→ To increase tension and require the class to take on further responsibilities.	We now return to the roles of Food Minister **(TiR)** and her advisers. Show the advisers the public information leaflet on household pets **(WR3, p. 187)** and insist that the advisers read the pamphlet very carefully before saying anything. Then ask for their comments. Explain that you are still deciding whether or not to send out this message and that you will carefully listen to the advisers' comments and suggestions before making your final decision.	
9.	Conscience alley	→ To examine the arguments for and against the decision to eliminate household pets	Having listened to the arguments class members are asked to decide whether or not they support the plan to ban and eliminate pets. **S.** They could do this by completing one of the following statements: a. We have to do this because . . . Or . . . b. We cant do this because . . . **C.** Alternatively they could choose their own words entirely. Group members then line up in facing groups of either a's or b's. It is quite likely that many (possibly all) of the advisers will choose to oppose the plan. If that is the case simply go down the line and listen to each argument as you pass each adviser. You might choose to go back down the line offering opposing arguments; e.g. *'Are we really going to put pets before people?'* It's not a problem if a whole group takes a unified stand but a counterargument does need to be heard.	
10.	Teacher narration	→ To move the narrative on → To create a context for further decision making and problem solving	You might wish to use this narration or alternatively to write/improvise your own. *'The Minister listened to the views of his advisers and (OR Despite the views of his advisers the minister) decided to go ahead with the pet elimination scheme. These were difficult times and difficult decisions had to be taken. When the people read the pamphlet the next morning they were shocked. They'd known there was a problem but nobody had expected this.'*	**Letters. Writing to persuade** Working as individuals writers are asked to write a letter in role as a pe owner to the Minister for Food. The letter is an attempt to persuade the Minister not to go ahead with the pe disposal plan. **C.** An additional task could be to also write a reply to the letter from the minister himself.

ctivity	Drama strategy	Purpose	Teacher guidance	Opportunities for writing
1.	**Writing/ drawing in role**	→ To explore how arguments can be forcefully expressed using simple images, words and phrases	In their family groups people prepare for a peaceful demonstration to save the country's pets. Make available large sheets of paper, cardboard, paints and marker pens and ask each family group to make a banner or placard to take with them to the demonstration. The placards or banners need to use words and images to make their point as forcefully as possible. *Should any family groups decide that they support the government's anti-pet policy then they can be asked to make a banner in readiness for a counterdemonstration.*	**Chants and slogans** **S.** Look at some examples of football chants and political slogans. Look how rhythm and rhyme are used to make effective chants and slogans. The brief for writers is to write slogans and chants which could be used to oppose the government's new policy on pets.
2.	**Still image (whole group)**	→ To share the work carried out on the placards and banners → To create whole group performance	Ask class members to stand around the edges of the space holding their banners and placards. One by one group members enter the space and adopt frozen positions gesturing or holding up placards or banners. Stress that this is to be a peaceful demonstration in which people are determined to make their point without using violence. Person by person the demonstration builds up. We could use a drumbeat to regulate the flow (e.g. a new person can enter the space on every third beat) and to build tension. Use a digital camera to record the final image.	
3.	**Soundscape**	→ To explore ways in which this moment can be captured and conveyed to others without use of visual representation	Ask the class to imagine that the group image they have just made is a scene from a radio play. The same intensity and meaning has to be conveyed to an audience through sound only. In the family groups they are now asked to find ways to express the same meaning using just language and sound. This will work well if they have already completed the 'chants and slogans' writing task (see strategy 11). The whole group soundscape can now be built up adding one group at a time.	**Eye witness accounts. Writing to describe** The task is to write an account of the demonstration from the point of view of either a demonstrator or an onlooker. **S.** Stress the importance of describing sounds and feelings as well as movement and action.

Activity	Drama strategy	Purpose	Teacher guidance	Opportunities for writing
14.	TiR MoE	→ Group members return to their planning and advisory roles with new responsibilities	The Minister **(TiR)** starts this meeting by showing the advisers a copy of a school lunch menu **(WR4, p. 188)**. It is clear that many children are getting an increasingly restricted diet while some families are still able to pay for some of the less available products. The Minister has decided that the time has come to introduce rationing. The advisers are shown a poster from WW2 **(WR5, p. 189)**. *'What is it trying to do? How have the poster designers used images and words to make their point?'*	
15.	MoE **Designing in role** **Still image**	→ To bring an imagined expertise to a design brief	In role as expert designers and working in their small groups the task now is to create a 3D living poster announcing a new rationing scheme and persuading people that this is the right thing to do. The experts can use their own bodies plus found objects to make their posters. Like the WW2 example their poster might have more than one image. It will probably use language and so a caption will need to be written to accompany the image.	**Captions** Each of the poster images needs a caption or slogan as well as an image. Look again at **WR5 (p. 189)**. Working as individuals writers must write a caption for the poster image they have made.
16.	**Performance (audience in role)**	→ To share and evaluate a range of responses to the design brief	The design experts must choose which of their captions they are going to use. Groups then take it in turn to show their posters and captions to the rest of the group. (Captions can be written on large sheets of paper or spoken by a member of the group as the image is formed.) We might decide to invite people to watch the display of posters out of role as themselves. **C.** Alternatively they can return to their roles as advisers when they examine the poster display with a brief to recommend one to the Minister.	**Evaluations (writing to advise)** Having seen each of the posters writers are asked to advise the Minister in writing on which should be chosen. **S.** The task can be supported by a checklist of things to include, e.g.: → Brief description of the image and caption.. → Three things we like about the image and/or caption. → Why we think it would work?
17.	**Essence machines**	→ To examine in a stylized way the fundamental change that the food crisis would create	In designing essence machines (see **Drama Strategies**) the class is given the opportunity to work in a more abstract and stylized way. Groups of three must capture the essence of a character or moment in a drama by choosing movement, sounds and fragments of language and then using their bodies to build a machine which repeats these elements in a continuous loop.	

Activity	Drama strategy	Purpose	Teacher guidance	Opportunities for writing
			The brief here is to make two contrasting machines. The first is called **Christmas 2012.** The second is called **Christmas 2024.**	
18.	**Essence machine performance**	→ To observe, discuss and evaluate each group's machine	There are a number of ways these machines can be 'performed'. We might decide to look at all the 2012 machines before leaping forward in time. Or we might want to examine the differences with each group showing their two contrasting machines back-to-back. **C.** Alternatively we might experiment with both approaches and ask the class to decide which is most effective.	**Play scripts** Working in their essence machine groups as script-writing teams the task is to turn their two Christmas machines into short play scripts which could be rehearsed and performed at a later point . **C.** Variants of this task could be to produce scripts for radio, TV or film.
19.	**TiR** **MoE**	→ To examine another moral issue from inside the fiction	In role **(TiR)** as Minister of Food remind your advisers that it is possible to pollinate some of the failing crops by hand. It would require hundreds of thousands of labourers and this solution has always been ruled out as too expensive. *'But now the army are telling us that there might be people in certain parts of the world who could be "encouraged" to come and do the job. It could be a very cheap solution because we wouldn't have to pay these labourers very much (if anything) and we could build simple secure camps for them to live in.'* You want to know what the advisers feel about this. Be deliberately evasive about how labourers might be 'encouraged' to come, why the army appears to be involved and what is meant by 'secure'. Don't mention the word 'slave' unless they do!	
20.	**Conscience alley**	→ To reach a group decision and to present that decision in a physical and visual way	Identify two areas at either end of the space. Label one area **'Yes to Pollination Labour Camps'** and the other **'No to Pollination Labour Camps'.** Group members still in role as advisers must walk to one of the two designated areas. Those who are unable to choose must stand in the middle. Discuss the issue again out of role and ask people to explain why they chose to go in one direction or another.	**Press release: writing to explain** If a majority of advisers decide to agree to the introduction of pollination labour camps then the brief is to write a press release explaining to the people why the government has chosen this route. If the decision goes the other way then the press release must explain why the government has rejected this solution.

Activity	Drama strategy	Purpose	Teacher guidance	Opportunities for writing
			C. After listening to each other's reasoning we might want to conduct the ritual again this time out of role. Are there differences when we make decisions as ourselves as opposed in role?	
21.	Reading in role	→ To introduce a new element into the drama which will require us to discuss key issues and make decisions	Ask participants to sit in their family groups. Display the poster **(WR6)**. Ask everyone to read the poster remembering that they are in role as a member of the family. When the reading has finished ask them to sit still and in silence for 1 minute and consider: *How does this poster makes you feel?* *What questions would you like to ask?* *What do you think you'd do if someone tried to sell you food?*	
22.	Thought-tracking (human keyboards)	→ To share family members' thoughts and feelings about the new poster	Standing in their family groups each participant must think of a word or phrase which is a response to the first question. *How does this poster make you feel?* Teacher now activates the chosen words and phrases by tapping group members on their shoulders. When tapped each person will speak their chosen words. Shoulders become keys on a keyboard . Interesting effects can be achieved by repeating the same 'note' or playing two notes at the same time. Invite members of other groups to play the keyboard. Experiment with two players (four hands) or three players (six hands). Repeat the process for the other two questions considered in strategy 21.	**First person narrative. Writing to describe and inform** The task is to write a paragraph describing a break-in at the food depot from one of the following perspectives: a. An eyewitness b. A security guard c. A food member of the food robbery gang **S.** Remind writers to think about sounds, sights, smells and most of feelings. **C.** Writers might undertake three back-to-back paragraphs describing the incident from each of the three perspectives.
23.	TiR	→ To confront the class with a moral dilemma and perhaps encourage people to reconsider some of their previous assumptions	In this **TiR** you are a black market trader talking to the whole class in role as family members. Using your own words or the following suggestion explain that you've got *'some very interesting food items at very reasonable prices. Some of the stuff is very rare indeed like sausages and steaks and fresh fruit including oranges and strawberries. And milk. Yes that's right.'*	

ctivity	Drama strategy	Purpose	Teacher guidance	Opportunities for writing
			Fresh cow's milk. When's the last time your kids had that? Don't listen to the government. They say we're criminals but it's the government who're the real criminals 'cos they're hording delicious nourishing food in their depots to feed their own families while ordinary people like us have to eat rubbish. What we've done is freed up this food to share it with the people. OK so you have to pay us. We took a major risk in getting the food out so we deserve to make a little bit of profit. What's wrong with that? That's just business isn't it?' Invite questions and discussion in role. Then pose the question *'So who's interested in buying?'* and immediately freeze the action.	
4.	**Improvisation**	→ To explore the issues raised by the black market trader from within the drama	Family groups now decide what they should do. Make sure that the poster **(WR6, p. 190)** is in view while these in-role discussions are taking place. **S.** You could suggest some options as a framework for the discussion. These could include: → do business with the trader → inform the authorities → do nothing and pretend this hasn't happened. Try to encourage families to come to unanimous decisions as this often promotes more intense discussion and argument.	
5.	**Hot-seating**	→ To reflect on and challenge the decisions which have been reached	By monitoring the decisions you will know which decision each family has reached. Choose a family which has decided to deal with the trader and invite them into come into the centre of the space while the other group members disperse around the edges. The family members stay in role while the rest of the group question them out of role. Ask the family to start by telling us what they've decided to do then invite questions and challenges from the rest of the group. Then if this option is available to you repeat the process with a family who have come to a different decision.	

Activity	Drama strategy	Purpose	Teacher guidance	Opportunities for writing
26.	**Still image**	→ To re-examine the decisions reached through a physical and non-verbal medium.	Working in their family groups the participants must now design a still image which illustrates the decision they have reached. It may show the food being purchased or eaten or it might show the trader being betrayed to the authorities. Offer to be in their images as the trader yourself if they want. If they decide to use you simply adopt the position they choose for you. Don't be tempted to direct.	**Diaries** Family members write their individu diary entry describing how the fami reached its decision and how 'we' feel about that decision.
27.	**Performance**	→ To share and evaluate the image work	Split the whole group in half. Invite one half to show their images while the others are visitors to the exhibition. Insist that the visitors study the exhibits in silence and do nothing to distract the group members who are showing their work. The viewing will last no longer than 1 minute and the viewers must think about how each group has made meaning in their image and choose one thing which interests them in the work on display. Allow the exhibits to relax before asking viewers to draw their attention to the things they found interesting. We will need to re-form individual images as they are discussed. Now reverse the process with viewers becoming exhibits and vice versa.	**Speech bubbles** Look at the way some comic strip writers allow their characters to talk by using speech bubbles. Using laminated speech bubbles and marker pens invite groups to supply speech bubbles for their own image They can then show the image aga asking people from other groups to hold the bubbles in appropriate places. **C.** The exercise can be repeated with groups writing bubbles for oth groups.
28.	**TiR** **MoE**	→ To provide one more dilemma for the advisory group to consider providing a springboard for further drama activity	Share with the group breaking news **(WR7, p. 191)**. You could stay in role once again as Minister of Food **(TiR)**. Ask your advisers for their response to this news. Inform the group that *some people are very angry that the Mantarak Islanders seemed to have misled the world about their honeybees. The Mantarak Islands could hold the key to the world food shortage and the headlines in some of tomorrow's newspapers will say that the government should use force to invade the Mantarak Islands and bring healthy bees back to this country.* The advisory group needs now to consider these four options: a. Write a polite friendly letter to the government of the Mantarak Islands asking them to give us some of their healthy bees.	**Letters. Writing to persuade** In small groups (perhaps compose on the basis of the views expressed in the meeting) advisers are now asked to write either letter 'a' or 'b' or the letter which the government would write to its own people if options 'c' or 'd' are chosen.

| | | | b. Write a stronger letter to the Mantarak government demanding their help and threatening action if this cooperation is denied.

c. Send an invasion task force to the Mantarak Islands to liberate honeybees for the benefit of the whole world.

d. An alternative approach altogether

C. You might decide to leave the drama at this point leaving the advisers to discuss the options without us or . .

S. You could stay in role and chair the discussion. | |
| 29. | **Still images** | → To reflect on the decisions made from an imagined historical perspective and to devise a visual representation of the outcome | Working in small groups participants are asked to imagine that 30 years have passed. In Mantarak the capital city of the Mantarak Islands a statue has been built to remind the people of the moment when the eyes of the world turned to their small island nation. The statue captures that moment in history. Does it show the islanders standing their ground and protecting their bees or sharing their good fortune with the rest of the world? Alternatively the statue might show the islands being invaded and robbed. The statues must show whether this was a moment in history which is remembered with pride or anger. | **History book. Recording the past**

The history of the Mantarak Islands is recorded in a book which is read by all the school children on the Islands. The final brief is to write the opening paragraph of the chapter which deals with the central part that the Islands played in the world bee crisis. The chapter is called 'The Day the Bees Died.'

C. We might point out that historical events are sometimes recorded and interpreted differently in different countries. An additional brief could be to write the opening paragraph of a similar chapter in a school history book written by an historian in a country whose bees had died. |

UNIT 7
Invisible

Introduction

This unit shows that we don't necessarily need dozens of roles to build and populate a whole-class drama. This unit about a lonely boy and his uncommunicative mother examines the obstacles to effective communication within the family. The activities enable a class to work 'inside' the fiction to explore the central relationship between Ben and his Mum.

Themes

- → Communication
- → Parents
- → Childhood
- → Family

- → Loneliness
- → Care
- → Love

Writing opportunities

- → First person narrative (alternative point of view)
- → Instructions
- → Message
- → Poetry
- → Evaluation
- → Questioning (framing and prioritization)

- → Diary
- → Character sketch
- → Advertising copy (writing to persuade)
- → Play script
- → Meeting summary
- → Play script
- → Memoir

Writing Resources (pp. 192–6)

- → WR1: Diary entry, Monday January 5th
- → WR2: Message fixed to fridge door, Monday January 5th
- → WR3: Diary entry

- → WR4: Competition entry form
- → WR5: Play script
- → WR6: School writing exercise

Other resources

Essential: Word slips, newspapers, a brief case, mobile phone, football scarf

Invisible

ctivity	Drama strategy	Purpose	Teacher guidance	Opportunities for writing
.	**Group reading**	→ To introduce this drama's two central characters and to establish their relationship	Read aloud and display diary entry, Monday Jan 5th **(WR1, p. 192)** Don't discuss the reading. Just ask the class to sit very still and think about what they've just heard/read.	
.	**Statement prompts** **'I wonder . . .'**	→ To establish an agenda for further enquiry and explanation	Tell the class that after reading this diary entry there are a lot of things which we know but also a lot of things we don't know. Sitting randomly in a space group members are now invited to identify some of the unclear and unknown things in this story opening by speaking sentences starting with the words 'I wonder'. **S.** Classes who are used to this strategy will need no preliminary help but if they are coming to this for the first time we might decide to model the approach offering, for example *'I wonder what Ben's Mum does for a living.'* Find a way to scribe the 'I wonders' for later reference.	
.	**Still image**	→ To examine and discuss the diary entry and turn it into a single image	In groups of three (two actors, one designer/director) class members are asked to recreate the diary entry text as a still image. Clearly a single image can't include everything in the text so groups will need to decide what to include and leave out. The image needs to sum up what we know (or think we know) about the relationship between Ben and his Mum. Tell the group that we are going to show these images in 5 minutes time and that they must think very carefully about where they are going to place their audience. In the devising phase the director can try out and evaluate the various audience proxemics.	**Imagined first person narrative (alternative point of view)** The task here is to write a brief account of the breakfast scene described in **WR1 (p. 192)** from Ben's Mum's point of view. **S.** Remind our writers that Ben's Mum would almost certainly have remembered the scene very differently.

Activity	Drama strategy	Purpose	Teacher guidance	Opportunities for writing
4.	Performance	→ To share the images created above and to experiment with audience positioning. → See **Drama Strategies**.	Groups need to decide where in the space they are going to display their image and where the audience will be placed. There are a number of options for audience placement. Here is an opportunity to try out and evaluate these options which could include: → Static audience in the round. → Promenade audience moving at will around the image. → Single 'camera' audience (i.e. audience bunched together and getting the same point of view (PoV). **C.** Double 'camera' audience (i.e. half group seeing the image from one PoV and the other half viewing from a second angle. Audience members can swap and compare the impact of the different PoVs.	**Instructions** The task here is to write step by step instructions for the staging of our piece of work so that people in a different group would know exactly how to do it.
5.	**C. Still image (abstract)**	**C.** To emphasize key elements in the relationship between Ben and his Mum using exaggeration and distortion	**C.** Here you might decide that this is an opportunity to discuss some examples of abstract and expressionist art and show how painters and sculptors have used form and line and colour to make meaning through non-realistic images. Ask your groups to see how they can use shape, size, height, facial expression, props and found objects to exaggerate and distort their image to emphasize the key elements of the relationship between Ben and his Mum.	
6.	**C. Performance**	→ To share, discuss and evaluate abstract images	This is an opportunity to discuss how the images have been changed and whether meaning has been added by the exaggeration and distortion.	
7.	Writing in role	→ To examine two new pieces of text and identify key words	Display and read aloud **WR2 (p. 193)** (Message fixed to fridge door, Jan 5th) and **WR3 (p. 193)**. (diary entry, Jan 6th). Place whole class into subgroups of six and give each group a paper copy of **WR3 (p. 193)**. Explain that in his diary entry Ben uses 132 words and that they need to sum up how Ben might be feeling when he writes that diary entry but choosing only 20 of his words.	**Messages** Tell the class that Ben gets lots of messages from his Mum. He keeps them all and puts them in a box. Each writer must now produce two messages to Ben from his Mum. Display the messages and perhaps later put them in a box.

Activity	Drama strategy	Purpose	Teacher guidance	Opportunities for writing
8.	Word collage	→ To turn an edited text into a sound/choral performance	Groups of six now experiment with their chosen words. Using some of the key 'tools' of vocal composition (see below) groups devise a vocal performance which encapsulates Ben's feelings at the time he writes that diary entry. The composition should last no more than 30 seconds. Groups should be encouraged to improvise and explore during the devising process. **S.** We could workshop some of these techniques with the whole class. Take a single word from Ben's diary entry and experiment with repetition, echo, volume, tempo, contrast, solo voice, ensemble voice, whisper, distortion.	**Poetry** Working alone writers must put their 20 chosen words on slips of paper. Encourage them to experiment with the slips placing them in different sequences and seeing how they fit together. Allow them to bring a limited number of 'new' words (say 10) which don't appear in the original. They must now have approximately 30 words with which to make a poem.
9.	Performance	→ To share the devised choral work evaluating content and presentation formats	Each group now decides on a performer/audience set up. Here are three just three possibilities: → Place the audience in the centre of the room and surround them with sound. → Place the audience at the end of the room and slowly advance towards them as the piece begins. → Sit the whole class randomly in the space with performers in among audience.	**Comparative evaluation** **C.** Each writer must choose two performances which presented the work in different ways and write a short review describing, comparing and evaluating the two presentations. **S.** Support the task by asking writers to answer questions such as: What were the main differences in the way the two groups used the space? What did we like most about each of the performances? Which of the two performances did we prefer and why?
10.	Teacher in Role (TiR)	→ To begin the process of building a whole group collective role and to 'meet' one of the two central characters in this drama	Whole group collective roles are very useful in developing a consistent shared understanding of a character (see **Drama Strategies: Collective roles**). Tell the group members that they are going to have the opportunity to meet Ben's Mum but that they only will only have 3 minutes with her because she's very busy so they will have to think very carefully about what they want to ask her. **S.** The time constraint is important here and we might need to help the group prioritize their questions in advance (see **framing questions**, writing opportunity).	**Framing questions** **S.** Working in small groups writers list all the questions that Ben's Mum could be asked. Then they must put rank questions in order of importance. Having discussed and agreed the ranking in small groups they must now work individually. Each writer must take a piece of paper and write on the top '*The most important question to be asked is . . .*' And then explain why they believe this to be the case.

Activity	Drama strategy	Purpose	Teacher guidance	Opportunities for writing
			Before taking on the **TiR** as Ben's Mum you will need to decide on a few personal details for the role and bear these in mind in case you are asked (e.g. her name, age, job, other children?). However although you will need to supply a certain amount of information you should also aim to leave the group with plenty of stuff to find out. For example, should someone ask *'Where Ben's Dad?'* the best response is *'I don't want to talk about that.'* It's important in this role to claim that Ben is very happy while at the same time providing some evidence that he may not be, e.g. *'Yes he is very quiet but that's just because he's a thoughtful boy. Doesn't mean he's unhappy.'*	
11.	Hot-seating (small group collective role)	→ To begin the process of handing over ownership and responsibility for a role to the members of the group	After a few minutes make your apologies and exit the role. Out of role discuss the character that the group has just met and evaluate the questions asked: *'How did we get on? Did we ask the right questions? Does she really understand Ben? Is she telling us the truth?* Then explain that they are going to have another chance to meet her but this time some of the group will join us in the role. Ask for volunteers and invite about six to sit alongside us as a Ben's Mum collective. If they've never done this before explain that this will feel a bit strange at first but that everybody in the group must try to answer questions as if they were one person and not a group (e.g. we use the word *I* and not *we*). Then reactivate the role by saying, for example: *'My train was delayed so I've got another few minutes. Was there anything else you wanted to ask me?'* From here on try to do as little as possible and let the other members of the collective answer the questions. Sometimes in collective role work an individual can hog the proceedings so it might be useful to impose a rule here that no single member of the collective can answer consecutive questions. See ***Drama Strategies: Collective roles***.	

ctivity	Drama strategy	Purpose	Teacher guidance	Opportunities for writing
2.	**Hot-seating** (whole-group collective role)	→ To hand over ownership and responsibility for the role to the whole group.	Now ask the whole group to take on the role of Ben's Mum. Sit them all together at one end of the room and explain to them that you are now going to question her. **S.** Explain that although the role will now consist of very many component parts they should all try very hard to think and respond as if there were only two people in the room; Ben's Mum (the group) and the questioner (you, the teacher). In the ensuing 'dialogue' you can aim questions at specific members of the collective to encourage wide participation.	**Diary. Shared writing** Ben's Mum has a diary. It's very different from Ben's. **S.** Perhaps explain that people use diaries in different ways and look at some contrasting examples. In groups of four imagine what a typical page in her diary would look like and together write her entry for January 5th.
3.	**Talking objects**	→ To develop the role of Ben prior to 'meeting' him	Ask the group members to sit around the edges of the space. Explain that we are going to find out more about Ben by meeting and talking to some of the objects in his room. See **Drama Strategies: Talking Objects**. Having 'cast' and placed six objects in the space allow the rest of the group to question these six objects.	
4.	**Role on the wall**	→ To share a group's understanding of a developing role	When the object questioning process is finished it's important to audit what has been found out. To audit a developing role we can ask group members to write on post-its and fix them to three large sheets of paper with the following headings: → What do we know about Ben? → What do we **think** we know about Ben? → What do we still need to find out about Ben?	**Character sketch** Write a single paragraph describing Ben from one of the following perspectives: → My best mate Ben → My pupil Ben → My son Ben
5.	**Reading in role**	→ To introduce new plot element and examine alternative narrative developments	Display 'football competition advert' **(WR4, p. 194)** and then introduce the play script **(WR5, p. 195)**. Choose two volunteers to read the script aloud and then divide the whole class into pairs. You might decide to use or ignore gender when arranging your pairs. The scene will work either way. Allow pairs 10 minutes to read and re-read the scene.	**Advertising copy (writing to persuade)** Discuss the advert for the football competition. Look at the ways in which the writers have used words to make the prize as attractive and exciting as possible. *Do you think that everything in the advert is 100% true? Who are the writers trying to attract? What about the quiz question?*

Activity	Drama strategy	Purpose	Teacher guidance	Opportunities for writing
				The brief here is to write the text for a different reader's competition. In small groups writers must decide on the target audience, the prize, the competition itself and then write the text. If writers are using IT in this task then look at fonts, spacing, size and colour.
16.	Rehearsal	→ To encapsulate the scene by selecting and developing a fragment of text	Having read the scene several times ask your pairs to choose six consecutive lines from the script. These lines must sum up the relationship between Ben and his Mum at this particular moment. As long as the chosen lines are consecutive it doesn't matter if they come at the start, middle or end of the scene. **S.** Have an extract suggestion ready should pairs find it difficult to decide on one for themselves. Each participant will now have three lines to learn. Give our pairs 5 minutes to learn those lines and then ask them to set aside their scripts and 'block' (stage) the scene in the space. Explain that when the time comes for performance a table and two chairs will be placed in the centre of the space and that the audience will view the scenes in the round. Allow the group 10 minutes to stage and rehearse their extracts. Make available some basic props (football competition advert, newspaper, Mum's briefcase).	
17.	Performance	→ To share with the whole group the decisions pairs have made about line selection, characterization and staging	Discuss with the group how the work should be shown. There could be a random 'who's next?' approach or they might prefer to show their extracts in the sequence in which they appear in the script. Which do they think would work better? Having seen the extracts there will be opportunities for pairs to explain why they chose particular passages and for the wider group to reflect on the work they have seen.	

Activity	Drama strategy	Purpose	Teacher guidance	Opportunities for writing
18.	**Still image/ caption**	→ To use image making to focus more clearly on a fragment of text	The pairs can now distil their performances even further by choosing a single line from the scene which they think is very important. They will now create a still image to illustrate the line. The image could be naturalistic or more abstract. They will need to write the line on a sheet of paper and place it on the floor as a caption in front of their still image. The images can be viewed by splitting the group in half (image performers/audience) then reversing the process.	
19.	**TiR**	→ To develop tension and to encourage group members to discuss and develop their own narrative outcomes	Explain that you are going to go into **TiR** as Ben and that they (as themselves) will have an opportunity to talk to him. First though Ben has something he wants to tell them. At this point sit in a chair and put on a football scarf. Use the following script suggestion by all means but it is much better to improvise your own words to this effect. *'I couldn't believe it when the letter came saying we'd won. I've been excited all week. All my mates at school are really jealous. Don't think Mum's that excited. Don't think she really wants to go but she'll like it when we get there. Probably. Thing is though, I'm a bit worried cos she had to go in to work this morning. She doesn't usually have to go in on a Saturday but something came up and she had to go in. She promised me she'd be back by 12. It's twenty past now and she's still not back. The car's supposed to be picking us up in ten minutes. I'm not sure what to do. What do you think?'* Someone will probably suggest phoning her up and if so use your mobile to 'make a call'. Tell them *'she's not answering . . . its gone to voicemail.'* Ask them what message you ought to leave. Ask them if they think you should go without her when the car comes. Be confused and unsure. Seek their advice.	

Activity	Drama strategy	Purpose	Teacher guidance	Opportunities for writing
20.	Still images	→ To provide an opportunity for group members to develop their own narratives	Discuss story developments and our feelings about character. *Do we prefer happy endings or sadder ones? Try to think like writers. What do we want our readers or audiences to think and feel?* Here's their chance to write an ending to this part of Ben's story as this is a moment which could make or break Ben's relationship with his Mum. In groups of four make a still image clearly showing what is happening to Ben at 3.05 that afternoon. Is Ben at the football just after kick-off? Is his Mum with him? Or is Ben somewhere else alone? The image could have all four group members in it or three or two or just one. Use the football scarf to identify the actor playing Ben and the briefcase to identify Mum.	**Play script #1** Writers are now asked to turn the still image into a play script. **S.** *Look again at* **WR5** *and use that as a model for setting out your script.*
21.	Performance carousel	→ To discuss and evaluate a range of plot developments	Clearly now there will be multiple and contradictory plot developments. Show each of the images in a performance carousel (see ***Drama Strategies***) and discuss each of the options offered.	
22.	Mantle of the Expert (MoE)	→ To discuss, negotiate and decide in role	Cast the whole group as expert story editors. Explain that the story of Ben and his mother has been developed by a team of writers (you will need to decide if this imagined context here is film, TV radio, magazine photo-story, etc.). The writers have put forward alternative plot developments and now as editors they will have to decide which way to go with this story. **S.** You might decide to join the experts in role **(TiR)** as a fellow team or possibly if you think that the group will need some direction as the chair of the editorial panel. **C.** Alternatively you might decide to leave them to it and just observe. Either way you will need to set a time limit and tell them their bosses want an definitive answer by . . .?	**Meeting summary** Writers imagine that they have been asked to record the details of the story editors meeting. **S.** The following template might be useful. 1. Which story idea was chosen? 2. What were the main reasons why this story was chosen? 3. Did everybody agree with this decision and if not why not? 4. Was a vote taken and if so what was the result?

ctivity	Drama strategy	Purpose	Teacher guidance	Opportunities for writing
			You might find that some group members will bat for the idea their group presented in the carousel and reject any other alternative. It could well be that no consensus can be reached. In this case tell them that their bosses might be prepared to accept a majority verdict.	
3.	**Collective roles**	→ To reflect on the characters and their relationship in the light of the recent developments	Once a decision has been reached explain that you are going to be part of a conversation between Ben and his Mum later on in the day of the football match. Place two chairs in the space facing each other at some distance. On one chair place Ben's football scarf and on the other Mum's briefcase. People now decide which of the two collective roles they want to join and then go and stand close to the appropriate chair. If nobody chooses one of the roles (this can happen!) then you will have to take it on yourself. We now know what happened today and whether the day was a triumph or a disaster for Ben. Here is an opportunity for the two collective roles to speak to each other. **S.** It can sometimes help to get the ball rolling by supplying an appropriate opening line, e.g. *BEN: You promised you'd come back.* *Or BEN:'Thanks Mum can we go again next week?'* *Or MUM: I don't know why you're making such a big deal about this Ben.'*	**Play script #2** Writers can use the improvised dialogue between the two collective roles as inspiration for a scripted version. Explain that this won't be a verbatim account of what was said but a version based on memory. **C.** It might be interesting to compare different versions and ask whether being a member of one of the collective roles leads to bias. **Memoir** Share the school writing exercise **WR6 (p. 196)** with the group. Discuss the way in which the 7-year-old Ben describes his best day. How might that 7-year-old have described: → my worst day → my most frightening day → my funniest day **C.** . . . and leaping forward in time how might our 12-year-old Ben describe the events which have taken place today.

UNIT 8
Once They Get Started

Introduction

This unit uses a series of safe strategies to examine the theme of bullying from the perspectives of bully, victim, bystander and those who have a professional duty to prevent bullying. This unit explores the key issues through movement, sound and visual image and provides a wide range of opportunities for writing.

Themes

→ Bullying

→ Power

→ Fear

→ Safety

→ Inclusion/exclusion

Writing opportunities

→ Poetry (shared writing)

→ Captions

→ Play script

→ Eye witness statement

→ Diary entry (writing in role)

→ Radio news report (writing to describe)

→ Report (writing to inform)

→ First person narrative (writing in role)

→ Poster

→ Action plan

Writing Resources (pp. 197–202)

→ WR1: 'Once they get started' poem

→ WR2: 'Once we get started' poem

→ WR3: Eye witness report

→ WR4: Anti-Bullying intervention guidelines

→ WR5: Anti-Bullying school action plan

→ WR6: Anonymous (aged 13) diary entry

Other resources

Essential: Word slips, flip chart, marker pens
Optional: Drum, caption sheets

Once They Get Started

Activity	Drama strategy	Purpose	Teacher guidance	Opportunities for writing
1.	**Still image**	→ To introduce the theme of bullying	Explain that we are going to embark on a drama about bullying. Ask the class to suggest different ways in which people are bullied both at school and in the wider world. Make a list of bullying types on a white board or flip chart. Now ask the class to stand individually in a space with eyes shut. Read the poem *Once They Get Started* **(WR1, p. 197)**. Ask people to stand up and then read the poem for a second time. This time as they listen to the poem they must use their bodies to make a still image and freeze it. **S.** We might suggest that the image could represent a bully or the victim of the bully or perhaps someone who is an eyewitness to a bullying incident. Now give out copies of the poem and ask people to choose and underline six words which they think are the important.	
2.	**Choral reading**	→ To share and discuss the choices made by other members of the group	Read the poem for a third time with group members joining in on the words they have chosen. Discuss the results. *Which words were chosen by lots of people? Which words were ignored? Why do we think were particular words chosen by lots of people?*	**Poetry (shared writing)** Working in groups of four the brief now is to sequence their 16 chosen words into a new poem. If groups find that they have the same word more than once that's fine. They must use it twice or as many times as it's been chosen. A good way to approach this task is to write each of the 16 words on a separate piece of paper to enable groups to experiment with order and structure.
3.	**Performance**	→ To experiment with interesting ways of presenting the new poem to an audience	Working in their groups of four the brief now is to find a way to present the new poems. Encourage groups to think about volume, tempo and tone of voice. Audiences can listen to the new poems with their eyes shut just as they did the original.	

Activity	Drama strategy	Purpose	Teacher guidance	Opportunities for writing
4.	**Image making (large groups)**	→ To give everybody in the class the opportunity to contribute their own chosen word and image to a collective representation of the poem	Split the whole class into four subgroups. Give each group one of the four verses of the poem. This is their verse. Everyone in the subgroup must choose a word from the verse and come into a space one by one and make a visual representation (still image) of their word. Again it doesn't matter if the same word is chosen by several people or indeed the whole group.	**Captions** Working as individual writers the task is to write a pithy caption for each of the four verse images. **C.** We can impose a constraint here by telling writers that they must not use any of their chosen words in their captions. We can show the images again with captions displayed on large sheets of paper or spoken aloud by a member of the group.
5.	**Performance carousel**	→ To present and share the work of individuals and verse groups	The four verse images can now be shared in a performance carousel. An accompanying reading of the poem will cue each group's performance and provide a clear performance framework.	
6.	**Improvisation (devising)**	→ To represent some examples of bullying	Read the second poem *Once We Get Started* **(WR 2, p. 198)** and discuss the difference in point of view and meaning caused by changing the pronouns. Explain that although we can see that some sort of bullying is taking place there is much that we don't know about the incidents described. Split the four groups into half. The brief for the eight groups here is to improvise a short (30 second) glimpse of a bullying incident captured by the poems. It is important here that nobody actually takes on the role of the victim. All the group members are the bullies. The victim must be represented by an empty chair. Stress that none of these incidents involves physical violence. The victims are never touched.	**Play script** Writers turn a passage from their improvisations into a play script. **S.** Explain that in writing their scripts people may want to change things and write better lines.. **S.** Examine and discuss the format of some existing play scripts before writing.
7.	**Improvisation (performance)**	→ To examine the examples of bullying which have been shown	Place the empty chair in the centre of the space and invite each of the groups in turn to come into the space and present their improvisation. **S.** The discussion of the bullying incidents can be supported with questions such as: *How many different sorts of bullying have we seen?* *How do we feel when we watch these incidents?* *Have we ever seen anything like any of these in real life?*	**Eye witness statement** Using 'Bullying incident: eye witness report form' **(WR3, p. 199)** as a template writers must choose one of the incidents shown in the performance and describe it in detail.

Activity	Drama strategy	Purpose	Teacher guidance	Opportunities for writing
			Which of the incidents did we find the most realistic?	
			Which of the incidents did we find the most difficult to watch?	
	Thought-tracking	→ To develop empathy with a character	Explain that, as a class, we are going to look at a specific individual who has been bullied. Read 'Diary entry' **(WR6, p. 202)**. Ask the class members to imagine that they are the person who wrote that diary entry. It doesn't matter if some imagine the writer to be a girl or a boy or if we all imagine that different forms of bullying have taken place. The important thing is to imagine how he might be feeling as the diary entry is written at the end of the day. Imagine a word or phrase which sums up those feelings. Ask the group to stand randomly in a space and then start to walk in among them. As you pass in front of a group member he must speak aloud the chosen word or phrase.	
			C. You can give this work more texture by moving faster or slower or by inviting class members to join you in cueing the thought-tracking.	
.	**Improvisation** **Eavesdropping**	→ To create multiple versions of the bullying referred to in the diary entry	Everybody in the class now imagines that they have seen the diary writer being bullied. Working in pairs they tell each other what they have seen describing incidents, sharing information and discussing their feelings. Stress that it doesn't matter if some pairs are talking about a boy while others imagine a girl or if different pairs have seen different types of bullying.	
			After a while ask everybody to freeze. Then walk around the space pausing for brief moments. As you stand still the nearest pair will reactivate their conversation freezing again as you move on.	
0.	**Forum theatre** See ***Drama Strategies***	→ To examine some of the ways in which victims can effectively respond to incidents of bullying → To evaluate some of the ways in which the victims of bullying can seek help from others	Discuss (as ourselves) the advice which we might give to the person who wrote that diary entry. **C.** Ask for a volunteer to take on the role of the diary writer. (We could decide to approach a member of the group in advance and brief that person on the role.)	**Diary entry. Writing in role** The brief here is use one of the courses of action suggested in the forum theatre and to create the diary entry of the day when the writer does finally tell someone.

Activity	Drama strategy	Purpose	Teacher guidance	Opportunities for writing
			S. Alternatively you could take on the role of the victim yourself in a Teacher in Role **(TiR)**. Either way the role needs to be a help-seeking role, for example: *'I don't know how to ask for help.'* *'Who should I talk to?'* *'What do you think I should say?'* *I don't know how to start the conversation. What's the first thing I should say?'* You can now set up a forum to test some of the ideas and advice which has been offered. Inviting other group members to join the scene as for example Mum, teacher, best friend, you can see what happens when the main character applies the advice given. As teacher you can freeze the experiments and ask members of the forum *'Is this working?'* *'Can we think of a better way for our character to say this?'* *'Might it be easier for our character if she changed the way she sat or stood?'* The actors can incorporate the suggested changes and the forum can then evaluate the results.	
11.	**Drawing in role**	→ To explore visual and non-verbal means	Stick sheets of flip chart paper on a wall and issue marker pens. Ask the class to think about one of the bullying incidents which you eavesdropped in strategy 9. The bullies have scrawled graffiti on a wall in a school or in a town but they have not used words. Just drawings and symbols. There's no writing to read but you can see only too clearly what they mean. You are going to create that wall of graffiti and find ways to 'scrawl' the 'hate' without using words.	**Radio news report. (Writing to describe)** Explain that television or print journalists would be able to illustrate their stories with film footage or photographs. Radio journalists must try to help their listeners to 'see' a scene using only words. The brief is to write a short radio news report describing the graffiti which has appeared.
12.	**TiR/Mantle of the Expert (MoE)**	→ To discuss some practical responses to bullying using roles which carry imagined responsibility and expertise	You will need to start by describing the role of the Anti-Bullying Intervention Team. Read the Intervention Team's guidelines **(WR4, p. 200)**. Who might these people be and what are their skills likely to be?	

Activity	Drama strategy	Purpose	Teacher guidance	Opportunities for writing
			Explain that your role **(TiR)** will be as Head of the Intervention Team and the class will take on roles as expert members of that team. Once in role explain that *'a school experiencing an outbreak of bullying has asked you to investigate the bullying and offer some advice'*. Start by examining the graffiti wall. *What is it telling us? How should we proceed? Who do we need to speak to first? What are our first instincts?* End this session by suggesting that the team takes a closer look at a specific bullying incident.	
13.	**Freeze-frame** **TiR/collective role/MoE**		Replay one of the performances in strategy 6. with an empty chair once again depicting the victim. When the scene has been running for a while bang your drum and ask the group who are performing to freeze. Study the final freeze-frame for a moment and then ask the whole class to resume their roles as members of the Intervention Team. Explain that they are going to have a chance to meet the victim. Here you can either: → take on the victim role yourself as a **TiR** → invite an individual class member to take on the role → invite a small group to take on the role as a collective → start off the victim role yourself as a **TiR** but quickly hand it over to an individual class member or small group.	**Written report. Writing to inform** Members of the Intervention Team must write a detailed report on what they have found out during the interview with the victim.
14.	**Soundscapes**	→ To 'capture' and communicate meaning using sound only	Groups of five or six are asked to create a soundscape* of a bullying incident. See **Drama Strategies: Soundscapes**. Their audience will listen to the performances of the soundscapes with their eyes shut. **S.** Imposing constraints and narrowing choice when setting the brief can actually help groups to choose appropriate sounds. You could for example say that the soundscape must consist of: a. words only b. found sounds only (no words allowed) c. mixture of 'a' and 'b'.	

Activity	Drama strategy	Purpose	Teacher guidance	Opportunities for writing
			S. Try to get groups to think about the 'shape' of their soundscapes. *Where will the sounds come from? Where will the audience be when they hear the work? Will the soundscape performers move around or stay still?*	
15.	Performance	→ To share the soundscapes and evaluate each group's use of sound effects and audience proxemics	Ask each performing group to place their audience and then ask the listeners to close their eyes. The end of the performance can be signed by the performers clapping. (Hopefully members will now open their eyes and join the applause!). Ask individual members to describe their experiences. **S.** *How did we feel when we were listening to it? Which particular sounds had the most impact? Did pictures of the incident come into our head while we were listening? Can anybody tell me about an imagined image? Would anybody like to ask the group who has performed a question.*	**First person narrative. Writing in role** Writers are asked to describe a bullying incident from a victim's perspective using as many references to sounds as possible. **S.** We might offer the following opening as a writing prompt. *'I shut my eyes but I couldn't shut my ears. It all started again and I could hear everything . . .'*
16.	TiR MoE	→ To examine some of the ways in which bullies seek to excuse their conduct and deflect responsibility for their actions	Replay one of the bullying incidents from strategy 6. (Perhaps use a different one from strategy 13.) Explain that you now are going to take on a **TiR** as one of the bullies in the group. The class now has an opportunity to question the bully from the perspective of their expert roles as members of the Anti-Bullying Intervention Team. **S.** Before starting this scene we might want to remind the class of the Bullying Team's guidelines as set out in **WR4 (p. 200)**. Start the scene by sitting down in role as the bully. Adopt a position of casual innocence. *'It was all a bit of fun. Some people can't take a joke. I didn't say/do anything wrong. It was other people mainly. This is all a big fuss about nothing.'* Admit nothing. Accept no responsibility for causing any hurt. If the experts start to become angry or frustrated the **TiR** might get sulky and clam up. This might be a good time to freeze the action for reflection.	

ctivity	Drama strategy	Purpose	Teacher guidance	Opportunities for writing
7.	**Forum theatre**	→ To look at constructive ways of challenging the bully	Invite the class (out of role) to reflect on the scene which has just been played out. Urge them to think about their role as anti-bullying experts. *How did that go? How did the experts get on? Were they getting through to him/her? Did they follow the guidelines in* **WR4**? *What might they have said instead?* Explain that there will now be another opportunity to go back to talk to the bully. This time a smaller group of experts will talk to the bully. How many experts should meet with the bully *(One? Two? Small group? Whole group?). If it's to be a smaller group who should be part of it?* **S.** Encourage the class to discuss body language, where the experts sit in relation to the interviewer and tone of voice as well as the questions asked. The experts can meet the bully again armed with suggestions from the class. The forum can now be used to run the scene several times with regular freezes to examine and evaluate different approaches. (Without ever breaking down and miraculously accepting full responsibility for the bullying the **TiR** can reward sensitive questioning and constructive advice by opening up a little.) At each break the question needs to be asked: *'How are they doing? What could be changed/ improved?'* Other class members can be invited to join or replace the experts in the forum.	
3.	**Writing and designing in role**	→ To use what we have found out about these bullying incidents to reflect on constructive anti-bullying action	In groups of four *(see writing opportunity)* the task here is to design a still image to feature on the anti-bullying poster based on the message and text which they have already written.	**Poster** Working in groups of four (in role as experts) the task is to write the text of an anti-bullying poster to be displayed in schools. The poster needs to: → have high impact → appeal to a specific age range → have a clear message

Activity	Drama strategy	Purpose	Teacher guidance	Opportunities for writing
19.	MoE	→ To discuss in role the practical steps which can be taken to protect pupils in schools from bullying	Inform the Anti-Bullying Team that they are going to present their ideas for challenging bullying in school to the head teacher who invited them in. In groups of four ask the experts to discuss clear practical steps which the school could take to address their issues. We might want to draw their attention to the Anti-Bullying School Action Plan pro-forma **(WR5, p. 201)**. All groups must come up with three key recommendations for the school.	
20.	MoE/TiR	→ To share and evaluate anti-bullying ideas	After the small groups have decided on their key recommendations set up a meeting between the head teacher **(TiR)** and the experts. Thank the team for their hard work and tell them that you are eager to hear their ideas. Group by group the experts will share their recommendations. It doesn't matter if groups come up with the same recommendation; this merely emphasizes that idea's relevance. It's important to find a way to scribe the suggestions. At the end of the scene thank the experts and say that you are looking forward to receiving their ideas in writing.	**Report/action plan** Working individually writers produce a written document for the head teacher in two parts. **1. Report** This section briefly recounts some of the incidents of bullying which the team came across. **2. Action plan** This section lists some of the action which the school needs to consider.

PART 3
WRITING RESOURCES

Introduction

Over 50 original writing resources have been specifically created to support the drama units in this book. They cover a wide range of writing types and can be used not only within these drama units but also as freestanding models for writing in other lessons if required.

Full-sized versions of all writing resources are available for download on the companion website. Where relevant, colour versions are available.

The writing resources have been designed to

→ support the drama units;

→ provide clear models of different types of writing;

→ introduce, sustain and develop narratives;

→ introduce and develop characters;

→ provide tension and focus;

→ present compelling problems to be solved and challenging dilemmas be confronted collaboratively;

→ act as possible writing frames for new writing.

Unit 1   Mary Maguire. Housemaid: Writing Resources

WR1: Housemaids 1890

Housemaids: England circa 1890
Source: photo-sleuth.blogspot.com

WR2: Mary Maguire poem

Mary Maguire. *Friday 9th February 1901*

Mary Maguire you're a maid of all work
And twelve pound a year is your pay.
Though your hands are all red
And your fingers have bled
For some reason you're smiling today.

It's still dark outside when you carry the coal
To the fire by your mistress's bed.
You work on all fours
While the mistress still snores
But a song spins around in your head.

The Housekeeper sends you to scrub the stone floor
And tells you to sweep the front stair.
Then it's chopping and baking
And though your back's aching
You smile like you haven't a care.

The mistress comes down for her breakfast at ten
And complains that the postman is late.
You serve her the toast
While she waits for her post
And you smile as you pick up her plate.

Then down in the laundry at half past eleven
You're rinsing the soap from a sheet.
Though the hot water burns
As the mangle wheel turns
You could dance through the steam and the heat.

And when luncheon is served you're at table again
As you dish out the mistress' pie.
Though she'll shout and she'll scold
'Cos her parsnips are cold
There's a twinkle of joy in your eye.

Then you beat all the carpets from two until four
Polish silver in late afternoon.
And you pause for a while
As you study the smile
On your face in the back of a spoon.

At evening more coal must be fetched from the yard
There are lamps to be lit on the way.
Housekeeper's in bed
So you butter your bread
And sit down for the first time today.

But you're not smiling now as you sip your sweet tea
And his words spin around in your head.
Though all post is forbidden
A letter is hidden
In the box that lies under your bed.

Mary Maguire you're a maid of all work
And twelve pound a year is your pay.
When you look at the door
You're not sure any more
And those smiles have all withered away.

Rob John

Inspiring Writing Through Drama 2012 © Patrice Baldwin and Rob John

WR3: Domestic service 1897 – some facts

Domestic Service in the Nineteenth Century

▷ Throughout the 19th Century till the First World War more women in England worked as domestic servants than in any other job

▷ In 1897 1.5 million people in Britain worked as domestic servants

▷ This equates to 16% of the working population

▷ In 1873 a housemaid worked from 6am to 10 pm.

▷ She would be allowed 4 hours rest during her working day so she would actually work 12 hours each day

▷ A housemaid would be expected to work six days a week plus Sunday mornings

▷ Most housemaids worked an eighty hour week

▷ Whereas women who worked in factories could make friends with other workers the life of domestic servants particularly in the smaller houses was often very lonely

▷ Women who worked in factories had the opportunity to meet men, form relationships and get married. Women who worked as domestic servants had very little opportunity to meet men.

Source: The Annals of Labour. Autobiographies of British Working Class People
(John Burdett: Indiana University Press, 1974).

HEXINGHAM HALL
RULES FOR DOMESTIC STAFF
SEPTEMBER 1900

1. WHEN BEING SPOKEN TO BY LADIES AND GENTLEMEN KEEP YOUR HANDS STILL AND LOOK POLITELY AT THE PERSON WHO IS SPEAKING TO YOU.

2. SPEAK AS LITTLE AS POSSIBLE. NEVER LET YOUR VOICE BE HEARD BY A LADY OR GENTLEMAN OF THE HOUSEHOLD UNLESS THEY HAVE SPOKEN TO YOU FIRST.

3. IF YOU ARE REQUIRED TO SPEAK YOU MUST SPEAK QUIETLY.

4. NEVER OFFER A LADY OR GENTLEMAN YOUR OPINION.

5. GENTLEMEN OF ANY AGE SHOULD ALWAYS BE ADDRESSED AS 'SIR'; LADIES AS 'MA'AM' OR 'MISS'.

6. IF YOU ARE REQUIRED TO HAND ANY OBJECT SUCH AS A LETTER OR A DROPPED HANDKERCHIEF TO A LADY OR GENTLEMAN OF THE HOUSE YOU MUST FIRST PLACE THE OBJECT ON A SILVER PLATE. NEVER PASS AN OBJECT TO A LADY OR GENTLEMAN FROM YOUR OWN HAND.

7. ALWAYS STEP ASIDE FOR YOUR BETTERS. IF YOU ARE APPROACHED BY A LADY OR GENTLEMAN ON A LANDING, STAIRCASE OR PASSAGEWAY YOU SHOULD STAND STILL AS CLOSE TO THE WALL AS POSSIBLE UNTIL THEY HAVE PASSED YOU.

8. IF YOU ARE REQUIRED TO CARRY PACKAGES OR CASES FOR A LADY OR GENTLEMAN YOU MUST ALWAYS WALK A FEW PACES BEHIND THEM.

9. YOU ARE NOT ALLOWED TO RECEIVE VISITORS TO THE HOUSE.

10. 'FOLLOWERS' ARE STRICTLY FORBIDDEN. ANY FEMALE MEMBER OF STAFF FOUND TO BE COURTING WILL BE INSTANTLY DISMISSED.

11. MEMBERS OF STAFF ARE FORBIDDEN TO RECEIVE ANY POST. LETTERS OR PACKAGES DELIVERED TO THE HOUSE WILL BE CONFISCATED.

WR5: Mary Maguire's reference

Hexingham Rectory
Hexingham
Norfolk
12th December 1899

To whom it may concern :

Miss Mary Maguire has worked as a housemaid at Hexinham Rectory since March 1896. Miss Maguire who was only 14 when she came to Hexingham has been an honest and hard-working member of our domestic staff. Her polite and efficient manner has impressed Reverend and Mrs Blyth who are sad that she has decided to seek employment in a larger household.

Miss Maguire is neat, tidy and in good health. She has taken no time off for sickness since joining our staff. Her duties have included kitchen and parlour service and occasionally waiting at table. She has been adaptable and good natured at all times. Miss Maguire is highly intelligent for one of her station and although we here at Hexingham Rectory will be most sorry to lose her I have no hesitation in recommending Miss Maguire for future domestic employment.

Yours faithfully

Agnes Berry (Mrs)
Housekeeper

WR6: Advertisement for a housemaid

WANTED FOR LARGE HOUSEHOLD TO START IMMEDIATELY

HOUSEMAID

She must be respectable, trustworthy and hardworking with a very good personal character. About 16 years of age. Excellent references required. Wages. £12 per annum.

For name and address apply at the office of this paper.

WR7: Fragments from Mary's diary

Sunday December 11th 1900

Went to see the family today. It was my afternoon off and I walked to the village to see them. I took them some presents. Cook made some biscuits this morning and gave me a big bag-full for the little ones. She also gave me some cheese and a big piece of spice cake for Ma. They was all pleased to see me specially the little ones when they saw the biscuits! Ma made a big pot of tea and we all sat round the fire eating and talking Ma said how proud she was that I'd got a job at such a fine house. She said that I was very lucky to work there and that the money I sent home was helping to keep the family fed. Since Dad died it's been hard for everyone but now I was working in the big house everything would be alright. She made me promise that I would always work hard and obey all the rules. I promised that I would always do my best. I wanted to stay and sleep all night by the warm fire but at 3 o'clock I had to set off back. It was nearly dark when I got back here. I felt sad because the time had passed so quick. I hate this place. If Ma could see how hard I work I do not think she would call me lucky.

Friday February 9th. 1900

The letter came early this morning. I went down into the yard at 6.30 to let Mr Perks the coalman in and he was smiling at me. He said 'I've got something for you Mary Maguire.' And I said 'Whats that then Mr Perks?' And he said 'It's a letter from a certain individual.' My heart nearly stood still and I couldn't hardly breathe but I didn't show old Perks I was interested. I just said. 'Who'd that be then Mr Perks?' and he said 'I think you know full well who that'd be Mary.'
And he was right. I did know full well.....and I've took the letter up to my little room and I've hid it in the box under my bed and tonight when everyone's asleep I shall light my candle and I shall read it.

Dearist Mary

Exitin' news! Yestrday I told my Mum and Dad abut us.. I told them how I met you wen I come to build that wal in the gardan at the big house and I sed how luvly you was and how we torked and torked. I told then how we got on so well it seemd like we'd known each other for months. I told them that we'd been walkin out for a cupple of munths on Sunday afternoons but I sed it wos a secret cos you'd lose your job if anywun at the big house found out. Dont wurry they wont tell no wun. I told my Mum and Dad how you hated your work, how they treetd you like a slave up their and thye sed you shud pak it in. My Dad sed no wun shud be treeted like a slave in this day n age. I arskd my Mum if you cud cum an liv with us for a bit till you get a bettr job and she sed she dint mind. She sed findin work int easy but I sed you don't need a job cos after a wile we probbly goin to get marryd anyway an then you won't have to work no more. I think you shud pak in that old job at the end of the week. I think you shud tell that old lady to go an boil her head. What do you think? I think you shud pak it in now. When I wait for you by the gates on Sunday I want to see you cumin down that drive an carrying your case. Then I'll kno your gone for good.

All my love
Arthur

Unit 2   The King's Daughters: Writing Resources

WR1: Termly school reports

Winter Term School Report

Pupil: **Goneril**   Age: **12**

Tutor's comments:

Goneril is a highly intelligent and very accomplished pupil who has once again excelled in Maths, Science and English. She is conscientious, determined and sets herself extremely demanding targets which she consistently achieves. Despite her excellent record of achievement Goneril's behaviour has again this term given staff some cause for concern . She has a quick temper and has on occasions responded very aggressively towards both teachers and fellow pupils when she is unable to have her own way. She reacts very negatively to criticism and on occasions when teachers have found it necessary to correct or admonish her we have had to deal with angry outbursts which can at times be quite violent. Despite this, Goneril can be charming and good humoured when she chooses. She takes great pride in her appearance and has a wide circle of friends amongst whom she is clearly very influential.

Number in Class: **10**   Position in Class: **1st**

Winter Term School Report

Pupil: **Regan**   Age: **10**

Tutor's comments:

This has been a very mixed term for Regan. On the one hand we have seen yet again some outstanding achievements on the sports field. These have included three new school swimming records and her inspiring and highly competitive captaincy of our all-conquering hockey team. On the other hand Regan continues to lack motivation in the classroom and is easily distracted. She is undoubtedly very able academically and it is sad that her results have once again fallen well short of her potential. Her homework is rushed and often incomplete and in class she seems to lack the patience required to see a task through to completion. Regan does not respond well to adverse comments and will often sulk for long periods when criticised by her teachers. Regan has a good sense of humour but her teasing of others can sometimes go too far. She can be very sharp-tongued and I am sad to report that on several occasions this term we have had to talk to Regan about unkind behaviour towards other pupils although thankfully we have had no repetition of the very unfortunate bullying issues which we were required to address last term. Regan remains a frustrating pupil who apart from her sporting prowess has yet to make the most of her wide range of talents.

Number in Class: **12**   Position in Class: **10th**

Winter Term School Report

Pupil: **Cordelia**   Age: **8**

Tutor's comments:

Cordelia is a highly intelligent and very thoughtful girl who has excelled once again this term in art, music and languages. She is sensitive, perceptive, artistic and enjoys any activity where she is able to express her creative flair. In her art work she shows enormous patience and attention to detail and her painting this term has shown an exceptional maturity for one so young. Cordelia is a very quiet girl and although she is admired by other pupils who value and respect her opinions she does not appear to have close friends preferring on the whole to keep herself to herself. Although she is a kind good-natured person who is acutely aware of the needs of others she can on occasions be stubborn and wilful. She has a very clear sense of what she believes to be right and wrong and can be intolerant of other girls who take their learning less seriously. We are sad that Cordelia has, once again this term, refused to take part in school games and sport.

Number in Class: **12**   Position in Class: **3rd**

WR2: Message to the King's advisers

Date: 9th January
To: Members of the Inner Chamber

TOP SECRET

As a member of his Inner Chamber, His Majesty the King orders you to attend a special meeting at the palace tomorrow (January 10th) at 11 pm. At this meeting His Majesty will discuss with you a matter of great importance to himself and to the whole country. You are ordered not to tell anyone else that this meeting is taking place. As a member of The Inner Chamber you have helped and advised His Majesty for many years and he trusts you to keep news of this meeting an absolute secret.

You are ordered to come to the Palace South Gate no later than 10.45 pm.

Lord Secretary to the Inner Chamber

WR3A and 3B: Headlines from The Daily Realm

3A

The Daily Realm 10th January

Rumours Spread of Secret Palace Meeting

News is emerging that the king has called members of his Inner Chamber to a secret emergency meeting which will take place later today. An unnamed source has confirmed that such a meeting has been called but was not prepared to reveal why. A number of rumours are circulating about the reason why the King may have called this secret meeting.

3B

The Daily Realm 14th January

Nation Stunned by Ceremony Shocker

The King threw the whole country into confusion last night by announcing on his intention to divide up the kingdom into three separate states. At a ceremony broadcast live on national television the nation was shocked as a series of dramatic events unfolded.

3B

Vox Pop
After the ceremony people gathered in the streets outside the royal palace.
'I can't believe what's just happened,' said 25 year old shop worker Mary Kent.

WR4: Diary extracts, January 13th

Goneril

So now we know. The king is to retire and tomorrow morning he will divide up the land into three. All my life I've believed that as the eldest it would be me.; that I would follow my father and the rule the whole country alone. But now the old fool's decided. A map has been drawn and the three of us will each be given a share. But first we're supposed to stand up and tell him how much we love him..... in front of live television cameras! I feel so angry. So let down. I told him I was disappointed but I didn't dare tell him how I really feel. I really feel like I want to take his precious map, rip it to shreds and throw the pieces in his stupid face. But I dare not. I have to play his game. So my speech will be written. It will be the best speech he has ever heard.....and tomorrow if I am to be given a share of his kingdom then I will make sure that mine is the biggest and best.

Regan

It was brilliant. You should have seen the look on Goneril's face when he told us today that there would be three countries and not one. 'But Your Majesty,' she said. 'I always thought that one day I would be queen of the whole nation.' He just smiled and said 'This way is better, my dear.' I thought she was going to explode. At first I was worried because Goneril will make her speech first but now I can see that there might be an advantage in going second. I know I can make a better speech than her. She may be cleverer than me but I know how to perform. I know how to make things sound good. I know how to win my father's heart. No, I'm not worried about Goneril. It's Cordelia who bothers me. She's a strange, serious little thing but I've always suspected the old man loves her most.

Cordelia

I don't know what to do. How can he ask us to do this? He ought to know how much I love him. He shouldn't need to be told. My sisters are already at work preparing for tomorrow. Speech writers have been arriving at the Palace all day. They will see this as a game and they will do.....they will say.....anything to win. But what of me? Will I play my father's game too? I don't know what to do.

Inspiring Writing Through Drama 2012 © Patrice Baldwin and Rob John

WR5: The three speeches: word boxes

GONERIL	REGAN	CORDELIA
LOVE	PRIZE	POOR
MATTER	ME	SILENT
LIBERTY	TRUE	NOTHING
EYESIGHT	MY	HEART
RARE	I	BOND
GRACE	SELF	LESS
BEAUTY	JOYS	DUTIES
CHILD	SENSE	FIT
FATHER	DEAR	HONOUR
BREATH	ONLY	LOVE
SPEECH	SAME	FATHER
I	METAL	UNHAPPY
YOU	WORTH	RICHER
SPACE	HEART	TONGUE
WORDS	LOVE	NOTHING
HONOUR	PROFESS	HEAVE
ALL	ENEMY	LOVE
RICH	I	MORE
LIFE	TOO	BRED
HEALTH	DEED	RIGHT
LOVED	MY	WHY
FOUND	MADE	OBEY
POOR	NAMES	MY
BEYOND	OTHER	SISTERS
LOVE	PRECIOUS	CORDELIA
DEARER	MYSELF	NOTHING

Inspiring Writing Through Drama 2012 © Patrice Baldwin and Rob John

WR6: Extract from Shakespeare's King Lear

from Act One. Scene One

Enter Lear, Goneril, Regan and Cordelia

Lear:	Meantime we shall express our darker purpose
	Give me the map there. Know that we have divided
	In three our kingdom: and 'tis our fast intent
	To shake all cares and business from our age
	Conferring them on younger strengths while we
	Unburdened crawl toward death.
	.... Tell me my daughters
	Since now we will divest us both of rule,
	Interest of territory, cares of state –
	Which of you shall we say doth love us most
	That our largest bounty may extend?
	Goneril our eldest born speak first

Goneril:	Sir, I love you more than words can wield the matter:
	Dearer than eyesight space and liberty
	Beyond what can be valued rich or rare;
	No less with life, with grace, health, beauty honour;
	As much as child e'er loved or father found;
	A love that makes breath poor and speech unable
	Beyond all manner of so much I love you

| Cordelia *(aside)*: | What shall Cordelia do? Love and be silent |

Lear:	Of all these bounds even from this line to this
	With shadowy forest and with champains rich'd
	With plenteous rivers and wide-skirted meads
	We make thee lady.......What says our second daughter
	Our dearest Regan?

Regan:	Sir, I am made of that self-same metal as my sister
	And prize me at her worth. In my true heart
	I find she names my very deed of love
	Only she comes too short: that I profess
	Myself an enemy to all other joys
	Which the precious square of sense possesses
	And find I am felicitate
	In your dear highness' love

Cordelia *(aside)*:	Then poor Cordelia. And yet not so;
	Since I am sure my love's
	More richer than my tongue

Inspiring Writing Through Drama 2012 © Patrice Baldwin and Rob John

Lear:	To thee and thine hereditary ever Remain this ample third of our fair kingdom No less in space, validity and pleasure Than that conferr'd on Goneril. Now our joy Although the last not least.......what can you say to draw A third more opulent than your sisters? Speak
Cordelia:	Nothing my lord
Lear:	Nothing?
Cordelia:	Nothing
Lear:	Nothing will come of nothing: speak again
Cordelia:	Unhappy that I am I cannot heave my heart into My mouth: I love your majesty According to my bond; nor more nor less
Lear:	How, how Cordelia! mend your speech a little Lest it may mar your fortune
Cordelia:	Good my Lord You have begot me, bred me loved me I return those duties as are right fit Obey you, love you and most honour you. Why have my sisters husbands if they say They love you all? Haply when I wed That lord whose hand must take my plight shall carry Half my love with him, half my care and duty. Sure I shall never marry like my sisters To love my father all.
Lear:	But goes thy heart with this?
Cordelia:	Ay good my lord
Lear:	So young and so untender?
Cordelia:	So young my lord and true
Lear:	Let it be so; thy truth then be thy dower

WR1: The Grand Parade

In the middle of the fine city of Hamelin was a street called The Grand Parade. On this beautiful street were the best shops in the city; shops which sold the most perfect, the most beautiful, the most expensive things that money could buy.

Every day the richest people in Hamelin would put on their best hats and coats and order their coachmen to drive them to The Grand Parade where they would show off how much money they had to spend. They would walk slowly down the street with their noses in the air as their servants shuffled along behind them struggling with huge bags of shopping

Number 2 Grand Parade was a dress shop which sold the most beautiful silk and velvet gowns. At number 4 they sold nothing but hats. Very expensive hats. Number 6 was a cake shop where you could buy cakes of almost any size, shape or colour. As long as you had the money and at number 8 ......well you could smell number 8 from a hundred paces because they sold nothing but dark creamy hand-made chocolates.

On the other side of The Grand Parade at number 3 they sold beautiful shoes and at number 5 was the most famous flower seller in the whole of the city. Next to her at number 7 was a toy shop full of the most wonderful surprises and presents for children.

Right at the end of the street at number 89 was a very strange shop. Whilst all the other shops on The Grand Parade were huge and brightly lit with windows piled high with beautiful things, number 89 was small, dark and dingy. From the street you couldn't even see what they sold at number 89 but every day a stream of customers made their way to the shop because at number 89 they sold spells and potions and the people of Hamelin had always believed in magic

WR2: Poem

The Piper

1. Beside a river and a wood
   The ancient town of Hamelin stood
   Its happy people looked around
   And said 'This is a lovely town'
   They loved their church, their clean main street
   They loved their park where children meet
   They were 'the happiest folk alive. . . . . .'
   Until, that is, the rats arrived

2. Nobody knew quite why or how
   A million rats turned up and now
   The filthy brutes ran through the place
   Hid in your drawers jumped in your face
   They heard them scratching at the door
   They saw them running 'cross the floor
   From up above and underneath
   Came rats with pointed yellow teeth

3. The people said "This isn't fair"
   And turned their anger on the mayor
   "It's all your fault you useless clown
   You promised us a perfect town"
   "We keep the peace and pay our tax
   And all we get's a plague of rats"
   "You're finished here without a doubt"
   The mayor said "Wait…I'll sort it out.'

4. When?' said the crowd. The Mayor said 'Now!'
   The people said' So tell us how?'
   'We'll start a fire throughout the town'
   'You're going to burn our houses down?'
   'We'll flood the place and watch them sink.
   And that'll make the blighter's think
   We'll fill the whole town to the brim
   Its common knowledge rats can't swim'

5. 'You must be joking!' they all said
   The Mayor looked scared and scratched his head
   'Its quite a problem after all'
   'The problem is your brain's too small'
   'I promise I will find a way'
   'Too late' they said. 'You've had your day.
   We've heard your promises before'
   Then. . . . . . . .there was knocking on the door

6. The door swung open. He was there.
   With grim grey face and wild grey hair
   With a long grey coat down to the floor
   Stood a man they'd never seen before.
   What is your business in this town?
   The stranger looked them up and down.
   They nervously removed their hats.
   'My business, said the man, 'is rats'

7. 'Don't be afraid. No need to fear
   I'll make your rats just disappear
   They say I have a magic touch'
   'The mayor just coughed and said, 'How Much?'
   'My price? A hundred coins of gold'
   The Mayor said 'What!' His face went cold
   'A hundred coins? I'd rather die'
   'Right,' said the man. 'I'll say goodbye'

8. 'Wait', said the crowd. 'Don't walk away'
   'We'll find the cash. We've got to pay'
   The Mayor said 'Fine. I understand'
   And slowly shook the stranger's hand.

9. The stranger gave a mayor a look
   and from his coat a pipe he took
   Then staring strangely at the moon
   He raised his pipe and played a tune
   The crowd had never heard for sure
   a sound as strange as that before
   They said, 'That's one weird tune is that!'
   And then they turned and saw a rat.
   The rat crept forward in a trance
   The piper played his deadly dance
   And then another and another came
   All creeping slowly all the same

10. And suddenly the streets were full
    Of rats responding to the pull
    Of magic music floating down
    A woman said 'They're leaving town'
    The piper took them through the streets
    To where the wood and river meets
    And leaping from the river bank
    The rats dived in and slowly sank

Inspiring Writing Through Drama 2012 © Patrice Baldwin and Rob John

11. The people gasped and clapped and cheered
    As waves of rats just disappeared
    The whole town laughed except the Mayor
    Who watched the scene with hard cold stare
    One hundred coins of gold to pay?
    He shook his head and said 'No way!'
    'There is no need to pay' he said
    'Cos after all the rats are dead.'

12. 'The crowd were shocked and made a stand
    'You promised him'. ' You shook his hand.'
    'You cant go back. It isn't fair!'
    'Oh yeah? Just watch me,' said the Mayor
    This time no knocking on the door
    This time he strode across the floor
    He said, 'Relax. Don't be afraid.
    'I've only come here to be paid'

13. The Mayor said 'No' and raised his hand
    The Piper didn't understand
    'You know exactly what I meant
    And we're not paying you a cent.'
    'I earned that money fair and square
    So pay me now or else I swear
    You'll all be sorry wait and see
    You'll wish you'd never heard of me'

14. Now people didn't like that tone
    They turned on him. He stood alone.
    'Don't come round here and make a fuss
    It's not as if you're one of us
    Don't threaten us. Don't shake your fist.
    You're nothing but a terrorist!

15. The Piper turned. His face was grim
    As people turned their backs on him.
    'Alright,' he said. 'You've had your chance.
    So now I'll play a different dance.'
    He raised his pipe without a word
    And now a lighter sound was heard
    They heard him play but no-one spoke
    As every child in town awoke.
    The children got up from their beds
    The music ringing in their heads.
    The piper's tune had caught them all
    None could escape his magic call.

16. The children came from everywhere
    A woman screamed out at the Mayor
    'You've got to stop him. Please I pray!
    He's trying to take our kids away'
    The Mayor said, 'Look. Just stop. Just wait
    Of course I'll pay. Its not too late
    A hundred coins? Will that suffice?
    Two hundred? Three? Just name your price.'

17. The Piper looked round at the crowd
    They all knelt down. Their heads were bowed.
    'They're sorry now. How can that be?
    They broke their word and lied to me'
    And now they're pleading. What a nerve!
    What do you think these folk deserve?
    What's for the best? What should I do?
    What do you think? Its up to you.

Ending A

The Piper led them up the hill
The children followed him until
They went inside a cave and then. . . . . .
The kids were never seen again

Or Ending B

The piper smiled and said OK
I'll let them go if you will pay
The Mayor said 'Right. We know your type
Arrest him! Quickly. Take his pipe.'

Or Ending C ? .... Or Ending D.............. ?

Rob John

Inspiring Writing Through Drama 2012 © Patrice Baldwin and Rob John

WR3: Report form

HAMELIN TOWN COUNCIL

Rat Attack Incident: Eye Witness Statement

Name:	Age:	Occupation:

Where did the rat attack incident take place? ....
....

How close to the incident were you? ....
....

Approximately how many rats were involved in the incident? ....
....

What did the rat(s) look like? Size ? Colour? ....
....

Describe what happened during the incident. ....
....

How did you feel while you were watching the incident? ....
....

What damage was caused to property? ....
....

What injuries were caused to people? ....
....

How did the attack incident finish? ....
....

WR4: Minutes of meeting

HAMELIN TOWN COUNCIL

Extract from Minutes of special meeting held between the Mayor and representatives of the people of Hamelin, 26th June. 7.30 pm.

At 7.56pm The Mayor said that.....................

.....................answered The Mayor claiming that........

The Mayor disagreed. He suggested that..........

There was widespread disagreement................pointed out that...............

HAMELIN TOWN COUNCIL

WANTED
EXPERT
RAT-CATCHERS

**WE PROMISE TO PAY GOOD MONEY
TO ANYONE WHO CAN GET RID OF ALL OUR**

RATS

SIGNED: *The Mayor of Hamelin*

WR6: The Piper's testimonial

Office of the Mayor of the City of Bremmerhaven

To whom it may concern :

The bearer of this letter is an extraordinary man. Two years ago our peaceful happy lives were ruined when half a million poisonous green snakes arrived from nowhere and infested our beautiful city. No-one was safe from these evil creatures which slithered out at night and found their way into our homes. Thousands of our people were bitten by the green serpents and many died from their wounds. Our soldiers could find no way to kill our slithering enemy and our doctors could find no cure for its poison. We were in despair until the day a stranger – the bearer of this letter – arrived and offered to help us. For a hundred coins of gold he claimed he could rid our city of snakes for ever.

Some people laughed at him at first. Our soldiers had failed to kill the snakes with guns and rockets and high explosives and this man said he could overcome our enemy with a simple tune on his pipe. And he was as good as his word. Don't ask me to explain how he did it but the next morning the stranger played his pipe and our streets became rivers of slithering green as the snakes made their way out of our city. By nightfall there was not a single snake to be seen. Our enemy has never returned.

The people celebrated. They called the stranger a hero. They wanted to build statues of him. They offered to pay him not a hundred coins of gold but a thousand. He wanted no statues and he would accept only the hundred coins he had asked for.

We gladly paid him and I say to whom it may concern that although I do not know his name I say again with all my heart the bearer of this letter is a truly extraordinary man.

Signed:

The Mayor of the City of Bremmerhaven

Unit 4   The Lost Bag: Writing Resources

WR1: Village roles questionnaire

Name: ....

(for the purposes of this drama use your own name)

Age: ....

(all participants in this drama are adults)

How long have you lived in The Village: ....

....

(You may have lived here all your life or moved in more recently)

Who else lives in your house? ....

....

Do you have a job? If so tell us about it ....

....

....

Describe what you can see if you look out of your bedroom window ....

....

....

What do you think is the best thing about living in The Village? ....

....

What do you think is the worst about living in The Village? ....

....

Apart from your home where is your favourite place in The village? ....

....

Inspiring Writing Through Drama 2012 © Patrice Baldwin and Rob John

WR2: The Lost Bag

A. Although it had a name the people who lived in the village always just called it The Village. The Village was a good place to live. It had a . . . *(here list some of the features which class members have identified and placed during the mapping exercise)* . . . . and the people of The Village lived happy and peaceful lives

Then the posters went up and everything changed. People woke up one morning, opened their curtains and saw posters . . . everywhere. Stuck onto gateposts and front doors, nailed onto trees, pinned to the door of the little church, plastered over the front window of the shop, tied onto the climbing frame in the school playground and lying in the road on the main street . . . posters. All the posters showed the black symbol of the Ministry of Information and they all said the same thing . . .

B. For three days the villagers looked for the lost bag. They got up early in the mornings and searched together through the woods and fields around the village. In the evenings when they got home from work or school they searched the lanes that led into the village and when it got dark they lit torches and hunted though barns and old sheds. People talked about nothing else but the lost bag. At first they talked about where the bag might be but by the end of the third day when no trace of the bag had been found their thoughts turned to what might be in it and why the Ministry wanted it back so badly.

C. On the morning of the fourth day all the villagers woke up to find a letter pushed under their front doors. It was too early for the postman. Someone must have come with the letters in the night. On the top of each letter was the black symbol of the Ministry of Information. The Villagers picked up their letters and read.

D. The villagers were very angry when the second poster went up. What right did the Ministry have to block their roads? How were you supposed to get to work? What if you had a hospital appointment? Many villagers picked up their mobile phones to complain but found there was no signal anywhere in the village. Their landlines were dead too and their computers for some strange reason couldn't connect to the internet. They were cut off. Completely cut off. They'd been angry before. Now they were scared.

Inspiring Writing Through Drama 2012 © Patrice Baldwin and Rob John

Ministry of Information

LOST

in or near this village
a large black leather bag

A substantial cash reward
will be paid for information
leading to the safe recovery
of this important item.

Call (in confidence):
07772 829643 1777

Ministry of Information   07772 829643 1777

Ministry of Information

Lost Bag

Instructions

1. If you find the bag or believe that you may have information about its whereabouts you must inform the authorities immediately by calling **07772 829643 1777** or emailing The Ministry of Information on **Min-Info@Gov.com**

    All contacts will be treated in strictest confidence.

2. If you find the bag you must not under any circumstances open it.

3. Do not listen to rumours about the contents of the bag.

4. Do not talk to strangers about this matter.

5. At all times co-operate with the police and a Ministry of Information as they attempt to recover the lost bag.

⚠ Warning

Anyone who deliberately withholds information about the lost bag risks immediate arrest and imprisonment.

 Ministry of Information 07772 829643 1777

Inspiring Writing Through Drama 2012 © Patrice Baldwin and Rob John

Ministry of Information

For the attention of all residents of the village

As you know we have been looking for a black leather bag which was lost in or near this village last week. Our attempts to locate the bag have so far been unsuccessful and so we now need to extend our inquiries.

> **We are planning to search all the houses in the village tomorrow. Starting at 6.30am, teams of highly-trained soldiers with tracker dogs will come to your homes.**

You are instructed to co-operate fully with these officers and obey all their instructions as they search your property. We remind all residents of the penalties they will face for concealing information about the bag.

Ministry of Information 07772 829643 1777

Inspiring Writing Through Drama 2012 © Patrice Baldwin and Rob John

Ministry of Information

Travel Information

The Ministry has decided that until the bag which was recently lost in this village is safely returned, residents will not be allowed to travel outside the village. Roadblocks have been set up on all routes into the village and those attempting to leave will be arrested. The Ministry wishes to apologise for any inconvenience caused and assures residents that all travel restrictions will be lifted as soon as the bag is found.

Once again we remind all residents of the penalties they face for concealing information about the bag.

 Ministry of Information 07772 829643 1777

WR7: Where do you stand?

North	South
A. We have to trust The Ministry. They would not be taking this action without a good reason.	**A.** The Ministry have absolutely no right to do this to us.
B. You should always obey the rules. Rules are there for a reason.	**B.** Sometimes rules need to be broken.
C. We must accept what they have done and just be patient.	**C.** They can't go on treating us like this.
D. If people cause a fuss about this the whole village will get into serious trouble.	**D.** This isn't fair. We must complain and make as much fuss as possible.
E. I am not prepared to risk my family by taking action. I want to just wait until this whole thing blows over.	**E.** I am prepared to take action now. I feel I have no choice.

Unit 5 Lorry: Writing Resources

WR1: A message to the World

Give me your tired, your poor,

Your huddled masses yearning to breathe free,

The wretched refuse of your teeming shore.

Send these, the homeless, tempest-tossed to me,

I lift my lamp beside the golden door!

From 'The New Colossus': a poem by Emma Lazarus engraved on a plaque and mounted inside The Statue of Liberty, New York in 1903.

WR2: A message to the World

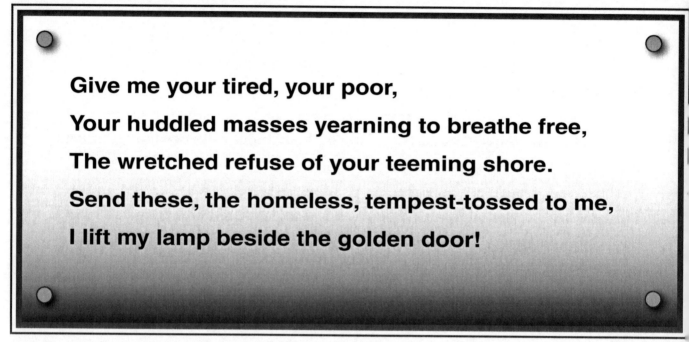

DANGER
PUBLIC WARNING

Travel not recommended.
Active Human Smuggling Area
STAY AWAY

From a sign erected near Mexican border. Arizona, USA, in 2010.

WR3: The People Smuggler from *Long Road to London* by Rob John: First performed April 2010

The Travellers nervously sit on the floor and listen.

Pay attention. What is going to happen now is that I am going to talk and you are going to listen very carefully and remember everything I say. Is that clear ? This is a very professional operation. My associates and I have been doing this for a very long time. We have helped many people to make this journey. We know what we are doing. You however have absolutely no idea what you are doing. Nothing that you have ever done in your lives will have prepared you for the journey you will start tomorrow.

This is not a picnic trip to the mountains. This is not a bus ride down the valley to see your uncle. This is not a holiday. This is your worst nightmare. You will be hungry but you will be too sick to eat. You will not sleep. Your body is going to hurt . You will be so hot you will struggle to breathe and within hours inside the lorry it will start to stink. After a few hours you will feel like you have entered hell. But this is just the start. You will have many more hours of this to endure. And it will get worse because when night falls you will start to feel cold. You think you know what cold is? You have no idea. This cold will turn your breath to smoke and eat right into your bones.

Then sometime in the night you will reach the first checkpoint. The lorry will be checked but remember this. Soldiers are lazy. They will only look inside if they hear a noise so you and your children will stay quiet. You will not even breathe. If they find you that is not my responsibility. You will have only yourselves to blame. So my friends are there any questions?

Good. Now. One last thing. See this?

He holds up a small suitcase

I need you to look at this case. I need you to look at it very carefully and study its dimensions because tomorrow each of you will bring with you one piece of luggage no bigger than this. You bring anything bigger and you don't go. You bring anything bigger than this we don't just leave your luggage behind. We leave you.

So don't try to pack up all your worldly goods. There won't be room for your worldly goods. You won't need your worldly goods because eventually after two days . . . maybe three who know's . . . someone will open the doors and you . . . will be at the coast. From there a whole new world is waiting for you and then my friends you will have all the worldly goods you ever dreamed of. Now go home. Pray. Say goodbye to your loved ones, summon up your courage and be ready for tomorrow.

Dear Mother and Father

By the time you read this I will be on a lorry heading for the coast. I know that this will be a shock to you and that you will be angry with me but I have decided that I have to get out of this country and find a better life somewhere else. I have been saving my money for two years and now at last I have enough to pay for my place on the lorry. I wanted to tell you of my plans but I was afraid that you would try to stop me.

People say there any many good places out there in the world; places where everyone has enough to eat and where people can live without fear. I'm going to find a place like that and as soon as I get there I will get a job and send you some money. Maybe one day you can come and join me there and we can be together again. Do not worry about me and promise not to be too angry. I will write soon.

All my love

WR5: Lorry poem (version 1)

1. There are fifteen of us inside.
   We don't look at each other.
   Like we're ashamed of being here.
   Heavy doors slam . . . it goes dark.
   Father squeezes my hand.
   I try to imagine his face smiling.

2. Then sickness.
   The stink of diesel and constant lurching.
   Father cradles me in the dark
   And wipes my wet face
   With a crisp white handkerchief.

3. We listen to the engine.
   Hear it gut-straining its way up twisting mountain roads
   Then screaming, free-wheeling down into valleys.
   Father opens up a bag of apples.
   I cannot eat.

4. At night it's cold.
   At first we sit alone.
   Strangers trying politely not to touch . . .
   But warmth slowly draws us together
   And we huddle in a tight shivering mass.

5. At the first checkpoint
   Father lays a finger on my lips
   We hold our steaming breath.
   Soldiers' boots crunch on frozen mud.
   Lorry doors slam.
   There's shouting in a language not ours
   And a dog barks.
   Then the engine starts. We move again.
   We breath again.

6. Twice more we are stopped.
   Once they open up the compartment.
   Shine torches at crates we hide behind.
   Light streaming in through wooden cracks.
   Surely they'll see us. Surely they'll find us.

7. Then on . . . picking up speed across the flat plains
   Heading for the coast.
   'The sea,' says Father,
   'Just goes on for ever. You wait. You won't believe it.'

8. And then, some time in the morning we stop.
   I can hear the cry of strange birds.
   'Seagulls,' says Father.
   We hear the driver leave his cab and
   Speak to someone in our language.
   He is laughing.
   As they open the doors
   We smell bread.

   Rob John

Inspiring Writing Through Drama 2012 © Patrice Baldwin and Rob John

WR6: Lorry poem (version 2)

1. We hid in a lorry.
   We set off in the night.
   I was with my Dad.
   It was very cold.
   My Dad held my hand in the dark

2. The smell of the lorry made me feel sick.
   My Dad tried to comfort me.
   We travelled for a long time.

3. Then some soldiers stopped our lorry.
   They were trying to find us.
   They looked in the lorry.
   We were hiding behind some boxes.
   We could hear their voices
   and see the light from their torches.
   We held our breath.
   I was very scared but
   They didn't find us.

4. We travelled right through the night.
   The next morning
   My Dad told me that soon I would see the sea.
   I had never seen the sea before.
   I was very excited.

5. The lorry stopped.
   I heard strange sounds.
   My Dad told me they were seagulls
   We had reached the sea.
   Someone opened the lorry.
   I could smell bread.

Rob John

Unit 6   When the Bees Died: Writing Resources

WR1: Shopping lists

Shopping List: 2012			Shopping List: 2024
New Potatoes	2 Tins Tuna	Bread	New Potatoes
Onions	4 Frozen burgers	Rolls	Swede
Tomatoes	4 Pizzas	Baked Beans	Parsnip
Green Beans	Pork Sausages	Biscuits	Turnip
Lettuce		Coffee	Lentils
Carrots	2 Tins chopped tomatoes	Chocolate	Bananas
Celery		Ice Cream	6 tins tuna
Brocoli	Minced beef	Wine	6 tins sardines
Oranges	Milk	Beer	Sugar
Strawberries	Butter	Diet Coke	Bread
Melon	Cheese	Sparkling Water	Bottled Water
Peaches	Yoghurt	Dog Food	Tissues
Avocados	Cream	Cat Food	Washing up liquid
Garlic	Corn Flakes	Tissues	Loo Roll
Spring Onions	Muesli	Washing-up liquid	
	Peanuts	Loo Roll	
	Almonds		

Ministry of Information

Food Shortages : Public Statement. 9.9.2023

Members of the public will be aware that due to the worldwide collapse of the honey bee population it has become impossible to produce many foodstuffs which we have enjoyed in the past. The Ministry of Food wishes to inform the public that from tomorrow (10.09.2023) the following food items will no longer be available for general purchase.

- All fresh and frozen meat products
- All dairy products (including milk, cheese, butter, cream and yoghurt)
- Most fresh fruit products
- Most vegetable products
- Coffee and chocolate
- Pet Food

The Ministry wishes to re-assure the public that plentiful supplies of rice, lentils, beans, bread, tinned fish and tea are available and so there is no reason why anybody should go hungry. We are working hard to find ways to improve food production despite the current difficulties.

 Ministry of Information 07772 829643 1777

Inspiring Writing Through Drama 2012 © Patrice Baldwin and Rob John

Ministry of Information

Food Shortages : Household Pets. 01.11.2023

Due to the current food shortages caused by the worldwide collapse of the honey bee population, the Ministry of Food has had to consider a number of ways to protect precious food resources. The Government regrets that as from today (01.11.2023) the production and sale of all pet food will be banned as resources must now be concentrated on feeding humans. Members of the public will understand that owning a pet is no longer acceptable in the current food crisis and to help solve this problem the government has set up Pet Rest Centres (PRC's) in all areas of the country. You are asked now to take all household pets (including caged birds, reptiles and fish) to your nearest PRC for humane and painless disposal. Members of the public are advised that from Ist January 2024 owning a household pet will be an offence under the Food Emergency Act 2023.

 Ministry of Information 07772 829643 1777

Inspiring Writing Through Drama 2012 © Patrice Baldwin and Rob John

POND STREET SCHOOL

School Lunch :
Today's Menu

Tuesday 25th May 2024

Boiled Potatoes or Lentils with Brown Rice

Tinned Fish of the Day
(today's fish is ....Sardines....)

Half a banana

Cup of Tea (no milk or sugar today)

Inspiring Writing Through Drama 2012 © Patrice Baldwin and Rob John

WR5: World War Two rationing poster

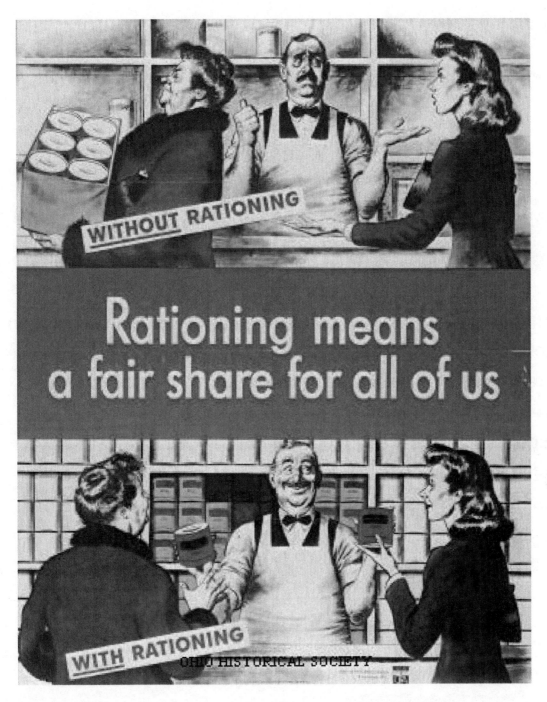

Source: © Ohio Historical Society 1943. Reproduced with permission.

Ministry of Information

SAY NO TO FOOD CRIMINALS

You may be aware that armed criminal gangs have recently broken into several Government Food Storage Depots and stolen precious food items including meat, vegetables and fruit. The government believes that these criminals will now attempt to sell stolen items to the general public. If anybody approaches you trying to sell you restricted food items you must immediately inform the police.

You are reminded that buying food from an unauthorised dealer is an offence under the Food Emergency Act 2023 which can result in a lengthy prison sentence.

- **Do not support food crime.**
- **Help the government to protect precious food resources.**
- **Say no to food criminals.**

Ministry of Information 07772 829643 1777

Breaking News

The government has this morning revealed evidence of healthy bee populations on the remote Mantarak Islands in the Pacific Ocean. The Mantarak Islanders who have for the past six years refused to allow visitors have always claimed that their bee colonies collapsed at the same time as those in the rest of the world. Spy planes however have taken photographs which appear to show honey production. There is also evidence that the islanders are successfully growing crops which are dependent on bee pollination. The government is holding urgent meetings today to discuss an appropriate response to this news.

Unit 7   Invisible: Writing Resources

WR1: Diary entry, Monday January 5th

January 5th

Back to school. Rubbish morning. Cold wet, dark. Mum doesn't even look up when I go down for breakfast. Just carries on reading her paper as usual. You can't actually see her when she does that. She's completely hidden behind her paper. I sometimes wonder if she's really there at all. Help myself to some cornflakes.

'I got football today,' I say.

'That's nice dear.' The voice comes from the other side of her paper. Yeah she's definitely in there.

'They're picking the team this week,'

'Good,' says the voice.

'Think I might be captain,'

'What?,' says the voice.

'Think I might be captain. In with a chance.'

The paper folds itself up and Mum's face appears above the headlines.

'Don't forget to feed the cat when you come in,' she says.

Go to school. Rubbish day. Football rained off. Have a test in Maths. Forgot all the stuff we did last term. Team pinned up on notice board. Not captain. Not even in starting line up. On bench. Sub. Rubbish.

Come home. Feed cat. Beans on toast for tea. Wash up. Do homework. Watch telly. I'm in bed when she comes home.

'Alright, Ben?' says the voice from downstairs.

'Yeah,' I say.

'Sleep well then,' says the voice.

'Yeah.'

WR2: Message fixed to fridge door, Monday January 5th

Hi Ben

Hope you've had a good day at school. Forgot to tell you I'm in London today and won't be home till late tonight. Plenty of food in fridge. Make yourself something nice. Make sure you do your homework and don't stay up too late watching telly. Hope you had a good day. I'll bring you back a present from London. Don't wait up.

Mum XXX

PS Don't forget to feed cat.

WR3: Diary entry

January 6th

Still raining. Mum already having her breakfast behind her newspaper when I get down. About to help myself to cornflakes when I notice she's used the last of the milk..

'I'm not football captain,' I say. 'I'm on the bench.'

'On the bench. Good. That's good .....isn't it,' says the voice.

'Not really.'

'Have some cornflakes,' says the voice.

'There's no milk,' I say.

'Well do yourself some toast then,' says the voice.

'Did you get me a present?' I ask.

The paper comes down and she looks at me carefully. 'It's not your birthday.....is it?'

'No but you said..........'

'What? What did I say?'

'Nothing,' I say.

She disappears back behind her paper.

'Got to go,' I say.

'Don't forget to feed the cat when you come in,' says the voice.

READER'S COMPETITION

Win the day of a lifetime!

Your fabulous chance to win the ultimate luxury football experience.

Prize includes :

▷ Two seats in a VIP box at a Premiership match of your choice

▷ A chance to meet top players from both clubs

▷ Pre-match lunch in a five star dining facility

▷ Half-time refreshments served at your seat.

▷ Travel to and from the match

All you have to do is answer the following question.

In 2003 David Beckham was sold to Real Madrid by which English Premiership Club?

A. Blackburn Rovers

B. West Bromwich Albion

C. Manchester United

D. Norwich City

Text / phone / post your answers to ....

Please note: entrants must be over the age of eighteen

Inspiring Writing Through Drama 2012 © Patrice Baldwin and Rob John

WR5: Play script

Breakfast time. Mum drinks coffee and reads her paper. Ben enters and sits down at the table

Ben:	Mum?
Mum:	What?
Ben:	I've got something I want to show you.
Mum:	What?
Ben:	I want to show it to you. You've got to look.
Mum:	Can this wait till tonight? I'm a bit pushed for time.
Ben:	You're not pushed for time. *(pause)* You're reading the paper. *(pause).* How can you be pushed for time if you're still here reading the paper? *(pause)* Doesn't look like . . .
Mum:	Alright! *(she the flings paper aside and glares at him)* What d'you want?
Ben:	I saw this in the paper. I cut it out.
Mum:	Football competition. What do you want me to do with it?
Ben:	I want us to enter. The prize is a couple of tickets to a match . . . of our choice?
Mum:	Our choice?
Ben:	Yeah
Mum:	But I wouldn't choose football. A match of my choice would be tennis. Wimbledon.
Ben:	You can't choose tennis. Tennis isn't an option. It's a football competition.
Mum:	You won't win Ben.
Ben:	I might. I know the answer to the question.
Mum:	Then I expect everyone else does.
Ben:	Can we enter? You have to be over eighteen. I've filled it in. I've done an envelope and everything. All you have to do is sign it and say you're over eighteen. If we won we could go together. You and me.
Mum:	I'd have to go to a football match?
Ben:	Yeah. With me.
Mum:	I don't do football Ben.
Ben:	Yes you do. I was seven. You took me. We went together.
Mum:	Did we?
Ben:	We played United. We lost but it was great. We had burgers afterwards.
Mum:	I don't eat burgers Ben.
Ben:	No but it wouldn't be burgers this time. There's a proper meal. Look *(he reads)* 'pre-match lunch in five star dining facility'. That'd be better than a burger. Wouldn't it?
Mum:	Ben, can we think about this tonight?
Ben:	No we've got to think about it now.
Mum:	Ben I really can't . . .
Ben:	Please, Mum. Just sign it. Please.
Mum:	Alright . . . alright. Give it here. *(Ben gives her the form, she scribbles on it, hands it back then gets up from the table)*
Ben:	Thanks Mum.
Mum:	Is that the time? Sorry I'm going to have to sprint. *(She grabs a briefcase and exits)*
Ben:	*(shouting after her)* Thanks Mum. I'll put it in the post on the way to school.
Mum:	*(from off stage)* Whatever. Don't to forget to . . .
Ben:	Cat. Right. Have a good . . . *(FX : The front door slams)* . . . day *Rob John*

Inspiring Writing Through Drama 2012 © Patrice Baldwin and Rob John

WR6: School writing exercise

My Best Day by Ben aged seven

My best day wos wen my Mum and me went to football. We got there urly and we had good seets. We were playing unitid and we lost. I didnt mind becos I was there with my Mum and we had lodes of fun. There was lots of singing and shouting speshally wen we scord are goal. We lost 2.1. Arfter the game we had burgers. My Mum dint like burgers so I had most of hers. She sed I had ate so much I mite burst but I didn't. It wos my best day.

Unit 8   Once They Get Started: Writing Resources

WR1: Once they get started poem

1. There's no stopping them
   (Once they get started).
   On the bus
   And In the street
   Hard cold mouths
   Spitting words
   At your back
   And sometimes at your face
   But mostly at your back.

2. There's no stopping them
   (Once they get started).
   On the toilet walls
   Scrawled in felt-tip hate
   With your name
   Misspelt,
   It makes you
   Wonder how
   And when you hurt them

3. You can only stop them
   (Once they get started)
   In your imagination.
   In there you
   Slash at them
   With razor words
   And watch them whining limp away
   All dripping blood and
   Strangely shrunk……

4. …..but in reality
   You're best advised to
   Fill your ears
   With sand and
   Button tight your lip
   And study hard your shoes
   And wait 'til they run out of hate
   'Cos there's no stopping them
   (Once they get started)

Rob John

Inspiring Writing Through Drama 2012 © Patrice Baldwin and Rob John

WR2: Once we get started poem

1. There's no stopping us
   (Once we get started)
   On the bus
   And In the street
   Hard cold mouths
   Spitting words
   At her back
   And sometimes at her face
   But mostly at her back

2. There's no stopping us
   (Once we get started).
   On the toilet walls
   Scrawled in felt-tip hate
   With her name
   Misspelt
   It makes her
   Wonder how
   And when she hurt us

3. She can only stop us
   (Once we get started)
   In her imagination.
   In there she'll
   Slash at us
   With razor words
   And watch us whining limp away
   All dripping blood and
   Strangely shrunk......

4. .....but in reality
   She's best advised to
   Fill her ears
   With sand and
   Button tight her lip
   And study hard her shoes
   And wait 'til we run out of hate
   'Cos there's no stopping us
   (Once we get started)

Rob John

Inspiring Writing Through Drama 2012 © Patrice Baldwin and Rob John

Mayflower Academy

Bullying incident. Eye witness report

Where did the bullying incident take place? ....

....

....

How close to the incident were you? ....

....

....

Approximately how many people were involved in the incident? ....

....

....

Describe what happened during the incident ....

....

....

How did you feel while you were watching the incident? ....

....

....

How did the incident finish? ....

....

....

Do you know the names of the people involved? ....

....

....

Mayflower Academy

Guidelines for in-school interventions

- We do not go there to punish or condemn

- We will learn nothing unless we gain the trust of the school's pupils and staff

- We must be prepared to spend more time listening than talking

- We accept that those who bully others may have been bullied themselves

Any recommendations we make must be realistic and achievable

Mayflower Academy

Anti-Bullying School Action plan

As school Managers we agree to:

- ....
- ....
- ....
- ....
- ....

As teachers we agree to:

- ....
- ....
- ....
- ....
- ....

As pupils we agree to:

- ....
- ....
- ....
- ....
- ....

WR6: Anonymous (aged 13) diary entry

Decided I was going to tell Mum. Today. Definitely. At breakfast time, probably. But I didn't. Didn't know what to say so I didn't say anything. She said ' Is everything OK?' and I said ' Yes, fine'.

Walked to the bus stop but didn't get on bus. Just kept walking. Went to the shopping mall and got changed in the toilets. Put my uniform in my school bag and wandered round the shops for a bit. Got no money so shops were a bit pointless. Went to the park and sat on the swings. After a bit I got hungry so I ate my sandwiches. It was only 11 am. Realised that a day's quite a long time. Quite a lot of time to kill in a whole day. Got a text on my phone but I didn't dare look. Didn't want to see who'd been calling....and leaving messages. Kept thinking about them back at school. Wondering what they're doing. Wondering if they're picking on someone else cos I'm not there. Went to library. It's warm in there and u can go on internet for free 'cept I don't go on it any more cos of the messages. I just read some magazines to pass the time. Phone rang again and everyone looked. Turned it off. Don't know why I carry it around. Might just put it in a bin. Get rid of it. Get a new one with a new number. Got changed again in library toilets and at half three I waited near the bus stop. Just mingled in with the others when it came. Nobody noticed me.

Got home and Mum said Good day? and I said Yes. And it was a good day in a way. Nothing bad happened. Problem is I have to do it again tomorrow . . . and the next day. Can't keep bunking off for ever. I've got to tell Mum. Or somebody. I'll do it tomorrow. Definitely. Probably.

Rob John

Inspiring Writing Through Drama 2012 © Patrice Baldwin and Rob John

References and Further Reading

Ackroyd, J. (2000) *Literacy Alive*. London: Hodder Murray.

Baldwin, P. (1999) *Parent Interview*.

— (2004, 2012) *With Drama in Mind,* 1st and 2nd edns. London and New York: Continuum.

— (2008) *The Primary Drama Handbook.* London, California, New Delhi, Singapore: Sage Publications Ltd.

— (2009) *School Improvement Through Drama: A Creative Whole Class Whole School Approach,* Continuum.

— (2012) *With Drama in Mind*, 2nd edn. London and New York: Continuum.

Baldwin, P. and Fleming, K. (2002) *Teaching Literacy Through Drama – Creative Approaches*. London: Routledge Falmer.

Boal, A. (1992) *Games for Actors and Non-Actors*. London: Routledge.

— (1995) *The Rainbow of Desire*. London: Routledge.

— (2002) *Games for Actors and Non-actors.* London: Routledge.

Booth, D. (2005) *Story Drama: Creating Stories Through Role Playing, Improvising and Reading Aloud*. Ontario: Pembroke Publishing.

Bowell, P. and Heap, B. S. (2001) *Planning Process Drama*. London: David Fulton.

Brindle, K. and Richardson, K. (2009) *GCSE Foundation English Revision Guide, new edn*. Glasgow: Collins.

Corbett, P. (2008) *Writer Talk, The National Strategies/Primary*. London: DCSF.

Cremin, Teresa; Goouch, Kathy; Blakemore, Louise; Goff, Emma and Macdonald, Roger (2006) 'Connecting drama and writing: seizing the moment to write research', *Drama in Education*, 11(3), 273–91, available at http://oro.open.ac.uk/9778/1/9778.pdf

Department for Children, Schools and Families (2008) *Getting Going, Generating, Shaping and Developing Ideas in Writing*. London: DCSF.

Dodge, L. (2011) *Email to Patrice Baldwin after D4LC Drama Lesson,* Little Snoring Primary School, Norfolk.

Dreyfus, S. (June 2000) 'Susan Greenfield: The Too-Much-Information Society', *The Independent* on Sunday, available at http://independent.co.uk/.

Egan, K. (1992) *Imagination in Teaching and Learning Ages 8–15*. London: Routledge Falmer.

— (1999) *Children's Minds, Talking Rabbits and Clockwork Oranges*. New York: Teachers' College Press.

Fleming, M. (2001) *Teaching Drama in Primary and Secondary Schools – An Integrated Approach*. London: David Fulton.

Godwin, J. (2006) *Using Drama to Support Literacy: Activities for Children Aged 7 to 14*. London, California, New Delhi and Singapore: Sage Publications Ltd.

Hall, N. and Robinson, A. (2003) *Exploring Writing and Play in the Early Years*, 2nd revised edn. London: David Fulton Publishers.

Harland et al. (2000) *Arts Education in Secondary Schools: Effects and Effectiveness*. Slough: NFER.

Heathcote, D. and Bolton, G. (1995) *Drama for Learning*. Portsmouth: Heinemann.

— (1996) *Drama for Learning: Mantle of the Expert Approach to Education*. Portsmouth: Heinemann.

Kempe, A. and Holroyd, J. (2005) *Speaking, Listening and Drama*. London: David Fulton.

Kempe, A. and Nicholson, H. (2007) *Learning to Teach Drama*. London and New York: Continuum.

Morgan, N. and Saxton, J. (2004) *Into the Story: Language in Action Through Drama*. Portsmouth: Heinemann.

National Strategies writing support materials, available at www.education.gov.uk/schools/toolsand-initiatives/nationalstrategies

Neelands, J. (1990) *Structuring Drama Work*. Cambridge: Cambridge University Press.

— (1992) *Learning Through Imagined Experience*. London: Hodder and Stoughton.

— (2011) *Beginning Drama 11–14,* 3rd edn. London: Routledge.

Norfolk County Council and National Drama, *Drama for Learning and Creativity (D4LC, 2005)* – action research logs of participating teachers.

Research for Teachers (2008) *Strategies for Improving Children's Writing Skills,* General Teaching Council for England.

Stowe, A. (2004) *Using Drama to Improve Creative Writing,* National Teacher Research Panel summary.

Toye, N. and Prendeville, F. (2000) *Drama and Traditional Story for the Early Years*. London: Routledge Falmer.

Winston, J. (2000) *Drama, Literacy and Moral Education 5 to 11*. London: David Fulton.

— (2005) *Drama and English at the Heart of the Primary Curriculum*. London: David Fulton.

Woolland, B. (2008) *Pupils as Playwrights: Drama, Literacy and Playwriting*. Stoke-on Trent: Trentham Books Ltd.

Index